Beyond Kübler-Ross: New Perspectives on Death, Dying and Grief

Edited by
Kenneth J. Doka and Amy S. Tucci

© 2011 Hospice Foundation of America®

All rights reserved. No portion of this book may be reproduced or transmitted in any form or by any means electronic or mechanical including photocopying, recording, or any information storage or retrieval system, without permission in writing from the publisher.

Ordering information:

Call Hospice Foundation of America: 800-854-3402

Or write:
Hospice Foundation of America
1710 Rhode Island Avenue, NW #400
Washington, DC 20036

Or visit HFA's Web site:
www.hospicefoundation.org

Managing Editor: Lisa McGahey Veglahn
Layout and Design: The YGS Group

Publisher's Cataloging-in-Publication
(Provided by Quality Books, Inc.)

Beyond Kübler-Ross : new perspectives on death, dying and
   grief / edited by Kenneth J. Doka & Amy S. Tucci.
     p. cm. -- (New perspectives series)
     Includes bibliographical references and index.
     LCCN 2011937383
     ISBN-13: 978-1-893349-13-1
     ISBN-10: 1-893349-13-6

    1. Grief. 2. Bereavement--Psychological aspects.
   3. Loss (Psychology) 4. Bereavement.   I. Doka, Kenneth
J. II. Tucci, Amy S. III. Series: New perspectives
series (Hospice Foundation of America)

BF575.G7B49 2011   155.9'37
                        QBI11-600169

Dedication

To Elisabeth Kübler-Ross, MD

A pioneer who ignited the conversation about death, dying and grief and set the stage for the pursuit of new thinking, research and practice in thanatology

—Kenneth J. Doka and Amy S. Tucci

To Dana G. Cable, PhD

Pioneering thanatologist, supportive colleague, and most of all—trusted friend

—Kenneth J. Doka

Dedication

Contents

Acknowledgments i

Introduction: Beyond Kübler-Ross: New Perspectives on Death, Dying and Grief — *Kenneth J. Doka* iii

Part I:
New Perspectives on Death and Dying 1

1. Strengths and Limitations of the Stage Theory Proposed by Elisabeth Kübler-Ross
   Charles A. Corr 3

2. Anticipatory Grief and Mourning
   Charles A. Corr 17

3. Task Models and the Dying Process
   Kenneth J. Doka 31

Part II:
New Perspectives on Grief 43

4. Does Coping With Bereavement Occur in Stages?
   David E. Balk 45

5. Positive Transformations in Response to the Struggle With Grief
   Richard G. Tedeschi, Lawrence G. Calhoun, and Elizabeth Addington 61

6. Beyond Kübler-Ross: What We Have Learned About Grief From Cross-Cultural Research
   Paul C. Rosenblatt 77

Part III:
Implications for Practice 91

7. Complicated Grief in the *DSM-5*: Problems and Solutions
   Colin Murray Parkes 93

8. Putting to Rest the Debate Over Grief Counseling
   Louis A. Gamino 113

9. From *Stage Follower* to *Stage Manager*: Contemporary Directions in Bereavement Care
   Robert A. Neimeyer 131

Index 153

Acknowledgments

Each year the Hospice Foundation of America produces a book in addition to its annual national program, while running myriad other programs, which has always seemed incredible to us. So this year—we decided to do two books and two programs! This is, in no small way, a testament to the energy of HFA's small but productive workforce. We are grateful for this opportunity to thank them and a supportive Board of Directors for all their efforts. Naturally we also need to thank all the authors who responded to tight deadlines. And, as always, we wish to recognize the continuing legacy of the late Jack Gordon, founder and former chair of the Hospice Foundation of America, as well as that of David Abrams—former president, current board member, and always friend.

Once again, it is wonderful to work with Amy Tucci. I am amazed at the synergy that we have developed. Truly this book benefits from her knowledge of the field, journalistic insights, and sharp skills. I am blessed by this most productive collaboration—and friendship.

My family, friends, and neighbors keep me grounded. My son, Michael, and daughter-in-law, Angelina, and my grandchildren Kenny and Lucy provide love and a push to play and relax. Kathy Dillon offers a warm companionship. I enjoy the ongoing stimulation of my godchildren—James and Austin Rainbolt, Scott Carlson, Christine Romano, Dylan Rieger, and Keith Whitehead and their families; and family, including my sister, Dorothy and my brother, Franky, (and all of their families) as well as good friends that include Eric Schwarz, Lynn Miller, Larry Laterza, Ellie Andersen, Jim, Karen, and Greg Cassa, Linda and Russell Tellier, Jill Boyer, and Tom and Lorraine Carlson.

I am also fortunate to live in a real neighborhood—one where people truly care for each other and enjoy opportunities to socialize. Neighbors such as Paul Kimbal, Carol Ford, Allen and Gail Greenstein, Jim Millar, Robert and Tracey Levy, Fred and Lisa Amore, and Chris and Dorotta Fields watch over my house when I travel and me when I am home.

Colleagues at the College of New Rochelle, the Association for Death Education and Counseling (ADEC), and The International Work Group on Death, Dying, and Bereavement (IWG) offer stimulation and friendship. I also thank the College of New Rochelle President Judith Huntington, Vice-President Dorothy Escribano, Dean Marie Ribarich, and Assistant Dean

ACKNOWLEDGMENTS

Wendi Vescio, and Faculty Secretaries Diane Lewis and Vera Mezzaucella for their ongoing encouragement and support.

—Kenneth J. Doka

To complete *Beyond Kübler-Ross: New Perspectives on Death, Dying and Grief,* seems an insurmountable project without the knowledge and work ethic embodied in Ken Doka, my co-editor. Ditto for Managing Editor Lisa McGahey Veglahn, who turned around manuscripts faster than most publishing houses would think humanly possible. To work with such professionals every day makes one's life richer, and yes, admittedly easier. My co-editors are passionate souls, and their dedication seeps into the work that they do—important work that undoubtedly improves practice and care of individuals and families faced with death and loss.

I would also like to acknowledge The YGS Group, our book designer, printer, and distributor, which works tirelessly to meet our tight deadlines and demonstrates extreme patience with edits and corrections at the 11th hour.

Finally, I would like to thank my dear family, Michael, Nicholas, and Rebecca, and my parents, Ann and Peter Stromberg, whose accomplishments and zeal for life inspire me daily.

—Amy S. Tucci

Introduction

Beyond Kübler-Ross: New Perspectives on Death, Dying and Grief
Kenneth J. Doka

Though individuals have written about loss and grief throughout history, the modern study of grief is often traced to Freud's 1917 influential essay, "Mourning and Melancholia." In his essay, Freud attempted to differentiate grief from depression. He developed the notion that in mourning one must work through powerful feelings in order to detach from the deceased, reinvest in life, and recover from and resolve the loss. A second strong influence was the work of Elisabeth Kübler-Ross. Since the publication of Kübler-Ross's *On Death and Dying* (1969), her stage theory has dominated popular thinking about the ways individuals grieve. While both Freud and Kübler-Ross's work had great heuristic value—spurring interest in the emerging field of thanatology (the study of death and dying)—much research since then has dramatically changed our understandings of both the dying and grieving process.

Yet evidence exists that many counselors may still operate from these older models (Corr & Doka, 1994; Doka, 2007) or unsupported assumptions (Wortman & Silver, 1989, 2001). Wortman and Silver (1989, 2001) suggest that many counselors adhere to the "grief work hypothesis." Their articles noted that the evidentiary basis behind such an assumption is weak.

In the past two decades, understandings of the grief process have changed in a number of significant ways (Doka, 2007). From:
- extending the understanding of grief from reactions to a death of a family member to a more inclusive understanding of loss;
- viewing grief reactions as universal stages to a recognition of personal pathways;
- seeing grief solely as affect to recognizing the multiple and multifaceted reactions that persons have toward loss and the ways that responses to grief are influenced by development, culture, gender, and spirituality;
- coping passively with loss to seeing the possibilities of transformation and growth in grief;
- relinquishing ties to revising and renewing relationships;
- seeing grief as simply a normal transitional process to recognizing more complicated variants and the necessity for careful assessment.

Ethical practice mandates currency in major areas. The goal of this chapter is to review the present state of grief theory and to discuss the implications of these new developments and insights for counselors.

NEW INSIGHTS AND DEVELOPMENTS
From extending the understanding of grief from reactions to a death of a family member to a more inclusive understanding of loss

Freud's (1917) case study of grief in "Mourning and Melancholia" began with a bride left standing abandoned at the altar. It is a mark of Freud's insight that in this early, influential paper that often is credited with beginning the psychological study of grief, Freud took great pains to identify grief with loss rather than with death. Despite that early perception of grief and loss, much contemporary work has emphasized grief as a reaction to death; however, this work does include an implicit notion of the many losses that engender grief. For example, *secondary losses*—that is, losses that follow a primary loss—have long been acknowledged as a complicating factor in grief. A parent who has experienced the death of a child may mourn not only the death of the child but also perhaps the absence of that child's friends. Rando's (2000) concept of *anticipatory mourning* also expanded the recognition of loss by moving the concept from mourning an anticipated death in life-threatening illness to a wider understanding that patients and families mourn all the losses associated with an illness, such as the loss of future dreams, present roles, and capabilities. This sensitivity to loss is evident in Rando's *The Treatment of Complicated Mourning* (1993), where she points out that both tangible losses (e.g., loss of a job) and intangible or symbolic losses (e.g., failure to gain admission to a desired college) may be grieved.

The concept of *disenfranchised grief* (Doka, 1989, 2002) also addressed the wide range of losses that engender grief, noting that many losses have been unacknowledged by the larger society, thus leaving individuals unsupported as they faced such losses. These losses might include the deaths of ex-spouses, gay partners, miscarriages, or even animal companions, but could also include other losses such as divorce, infertility, or job loss. Every society has "grieving rules." Generally these grieving rules emphasize that family members have a right to grieve the deaths of other family members. The concept of disenfranchised grief addresses that, in many situations—including losses that are not confined to death alone—individuals might experience a significant loss but be deprived of the opportunity to publicly acknowledge the loss, openly mourn, or receive social support.

This wider understanding of loss is buttressed by Boss's (1999) concept of *ambiguous loss* as well as Roos's (2002) notion of *chronic sorrow*, and Bruce and Schultz's (2001) concept of *nonfinite loss*. Each of these concepts deals with grief engendered by an ongoing loss, such as losses involving a child with developmental disabilities or a spouse or parent with dementia.

It is little wonder that Harvey (1998) suggested the need for a psychology of loss. For Harvey, grief then becomes a reaction to a particular form of stress—one generated by any significant loss. Mourning can then be seen to follow and to draw from more generic insights about crises, coping, and adaptation. If counselors use this view, they should be sensitive to dimensions of loss that emerge as clients cope with change and transition.

The danger here is that grief can become so generic as to be meaningless. Counselors need to be sensitive to the particular meaning that any given loss has for an individual. In some cases, an individual may view the loss of a job as one of minor importance or see it as a spur to retirement or education. For others, a similar job loss may be a devastating blow to one's sense of identity and meaning. Research that clearly describes the manifestations and processes of grief in losses that are not directly related to death can help establish a baseline for evidence-based practice, reinforcing ideas of which losses are or are not likely to be highly problematic.

From viewing grief reactions as universal stages to a recognition of personal pathways

Building on the early stage-based work of Kübler-Ross (1969), as well as Bowlby and Parkes (1970) and Parkes (1970), most of the early models of grief sought to find a universal set of stages that grieving individuals experienced. The original study by Kübler-Ross of adults with life-threatening illness reported that they coped with impending death by experiencing a movement through stages of denial, bargaining, anger, and depression to reach a state of acceptance. That schema was then readily applied by many to post-death grief. Stage theories were popular since they were relatively straightforward and seemed to promise a therapeutic protocol for moving grieving individuals toward some form of resolution. Neimeyer (personal communication, 2007) suggested that the popularity of stage theories lies in the fact that they follow an epic narrative long rooted in Western culture—the protagonist journeys through numerous obstacles, finally accepting his or her fate.

Despite the popular and in some ways continued embrace of stage theory, there has been a considerable disenchantment with stage theories. Notwithstanding a more recent study, highly disputed in methodology, assumptions, and conclusions (Maciejewski, Zhang, Block, & Prigerson, 2007), there is little empirical evidence for stages (Metzger, 1979; Schulz & Aderman, 1974). Moreover, in a field that emphasizes individuality and diversity, it seems naïve to believe that all individuals will cope with loss similarly or even choose acceptance as a therapeutic goal.

Worden (1982) broke new ground in his book, *Grief Counseling and Grief Therapy*, by conceptualizing mourning as a series of four tasks. These tasks are:

1. To accept the reality of the death
2. To work through the pain of grief
3. To adjust to an environment where the deceased is missing
4. To withdraw emotional energy from the deceased and reinvest it in another relationship. In the second and third editions (1991, 2002), this was revised to read "To emotionally relocate the deceased and move on with life," a modification that will be discussed later. The fourth edition (2009) states the task as "To find an enduring connection to the deceased in the midst of embarking on a new life."

Doka (1993) suggested a fifth task—"to rebuild spiritual systems challenged by the loss"—to recognize that some losses challenge personal spiritual belief systems, causing individuals to question and possibly redefine their faith.

Though Worden's tasks clearly identify grief and mourning with death, his underlying model represented a significant paradigm shift from the predominant stage theories. Worden's task model made no assumption of linearity. Individuals worked on whatever issues arose in the process of mourning. This theory stressed individuality. While facing common issues, grieving individuals could cope with these tasks in their own individual and idiosyncratic ways. One could have difficulty with one task and not others. Moreover, the model offered autonomy; survivors could choose when they were ready to tackle any task (Corr, 1992). Worden's work also prompted the application of task-oriented models to understanding the dying process (Corr, 1992; Doka, 2009).

Other models have also gained currency in the field. For example, Stroebe and Schut's (1999) Dual Process Model is often cited. This model suggests that successful coping in bereavement means oscillating or moving between loss-oriented and restoration-oriented processes. Persons who are fixated with restoration risk denying the reality of the loss, while those who focus only on the loss may be prone to chronic grief reactions.

Beyond stressing individual pathways in grief, both models reaffirmed that mourning was more than simply a series of essentially affective responses to loss. In addition, each of these newer models asserted that mourning involved not only a response to the loss of another but also an effort to manage life in a world now changed by significant loss.

These models offer much to counselors assisting bereaved persons. Stage models suggested a more limited role for counselors—interpreting the reactions of bereaved individuals and essentially assisting them as they moved through the stages. Drawing on these newer models, the counselor can take a more significant role in assisting bereaved persons in understanding what factors are complicating the completion of certain tasks or processes and helping to develop interventions that can aid them.

These models also have implications for bereavement support group programs and grief education. It is insufficient, and as later discussed, possibly deleterious, to simply ventilate affect. Grief groups and grief curricula should reflect the variety of ways that individuals cope with loss and examine all the processes and tasks inherent in mourning a significant loss.

From seeing grief solely as affect to recognizing the multiple and multifaceted reactions that persons have toward loss and the ways that responses to grief are influenced by development, culture, gender, and spirituality

While research from Lindemann (1944) on has always emphasized that grief is manifested in many ways, including cognitive, physical, emotional, behavioral, social, and spiritual reactions, much attention has been placed on affective reactions to loss, almost to the exclusion of other responses. Sue and Sue (2008) suggest that this reflects a general bias toward emotional disclosure common in Western culture.

Although a number of scholars have stressed reactions to loss that go beyond affect, some examples are particularly illustrative. To Neimeyer (2001), reconstruction of meaning represents a critical issue, if not *the* critical issue, in grief. The nature of a significant loss can create crises of meaning, challenging an individual's assumptions of identity, relationships, spirituality, and the nature of the world. The purpose of grief counseling is to understand the effects of loss on meaning and to help individuals coping with loss to reconstruct systems of meaning in the face of this loss. Neimeyer's work adds both a strong cognitive and spiritual component to the study of grief.

Doka and Martin (2010; see also Martin & Doka, 2000) adopted an alternative approach by originally beginning a study of expressions of male grieving. Their work led them to a different point—that of grieving styles that are certainly influenced by, but not determined by, gender. They have suggested a continuum of adaptive grieving styles ranging from the intuitive to the instrumental. Intuitive grievers experience grief as strong waves of emotion, and express and adapt to grief in strongly affective ways. Instrumental grievers, by contrast, are likely to experience muted affective reactions to loss, as their experience is more likely to be cognitive and behavioral in character. In adapting to loss, doing and thinking through the loss are most likely to be utilized by instrumental grievers. Doka and Martin's (2010) work strongly challenges the grief work hypothesis that only through the expression of inner feelings can someone effectively cope with grief.

Further, the concept that the processing of emotion is essential to healthy grieving has been challenged by other research. Bonanno (2004) suggests that adaptation to loss is facilitated when grief-related distress is minimized and positive affect is accentuated. Similarly, Nolen-Hoeksema, McBride, and Larson (1997) affirm that excessive rumination about a loss is associated with poor outcomes. Resilient individuals minimize rumination by both distraction and shifting attention toward more positive affect. However, Nolen-Hoeksema and her associates caution that deliberate avoidance and suppression of grief are equally maladaptive.

Beyond simply affirming the complexity of grief reactions, this research suggests that counselors and bereavement group leaders must move beyond simply processing anguish and loss to exploring effective ways clients can cope with the experience of grief. It also emphasizes the need for therapists to encourage the recognition of positive memories and experiences within grief. These concepts reaffirm the individuality of the grief experience—discouraging more dogmatic, "one size fits all" interventive strategies. This distinction is especially critical in light of recent work in grief that emphasizes individual differences and diversity in reactions and responses to grief based upon development (Doka & Tucci, 2008; Silverman, 2000; Worden, 1996); gender (Field, Hockey, & Small, 1997; Martin & Doka, 2000); spirituality (Doka, 1993; Garces-Foley, 2006; Puchalski, 2006); and ethnicity (Field, Hockey, & Small, 1997; Holloway, 2002; Rosenblatt & Wallace, 2005).

From coping passively with loss to seeing the possibilities of transformation and growth in grief

Early work in the field tended to emphasize the difficulty of coping with loss, focusing on restoring a sense of equilibrium in the face of loss while slowly and painfully withdrawing emotional energy from the deceased. The perception of the survivor was primarily passive, coping with changes out of his or her control.

This conception of the individual as a passive victim of grief was strongly challenged in the work of Catherine Sanders (1989). Based on research with grieving parents and spouses, Sanders found that most people followed a common sequence in the process of grieving. The first phase was *shock* as individuals began to feel the impact of the death. The second phase, Sanders proposed, was *awareness of loss*. As the shock receded, grieving individuals experienced an intense period of high emotional and cognitive arousal due to separation anxiety. Often the bereaved person became exhausted and needed to withdraw from others in order to conserve limited energy. Sanders then proposed *conservation-withdrawal* as the third phase of bereavement. This is a long, and for some people, an unceasing phase. Here the individual who is grieving externally seems to be functioning—returning to work and fulfilling basic roles and responsibilities. Internally, however, this attempt to re-engage consumes almost all the person's energy. The individual experiencing grief is often physically tired and in a chronic state of emotional pain.

Sanders suggested that bereaved persons face three choices when they are in this phase. Faced with physical and psychological stress and an immune system overburdened by chronic stress, some may consciously or unconsciously seek their own death rather than live without the person who died. Others may assume that the energy for major life adjustments requires more strength and power than they currently possess. They may choose to retain the status quo—living their remaining lives in a diminished state of chronic grief. Still others may make a conscious decision to adjust to their loss.

According to Sanders, bereaved individuals who choose to move forward often experienced a fourth phase: *healing—the turning point*. In Sanders's research, many bereaved individuals could actually point to a moment where they consciously decided that their lives needed to change. In one of Sanders's illustrative case vignettes, an older widow recalls hearing her young granddaughter ask her mother, the widow's adult daughter, "why Grandma always cries." The widow resolved that she had to do something lest she be remembered as the "grandma who always cried." In this phase individuals reconstruct their identities and live with an enhanced sense of restored physical health, increased energy, and psychological vigor.

Individuals who experienced that turning point moved to a fifth phase of bereavement that Sanders called *renewal*. While these bereaved persons still experienced occasional bad days and episodic moments of grief, such as at the anniversary of the death and other significant events, they now experienced a new level of functioning characterized by enhanced self-awareness, increased levels of energy, personal revitalization, and the renewal of social ties. At this phase, bereaved individuals have learned to live without the physical presence of the person even as they retain an internal sense of the deceased's presence. Sanders noted that in this phase bereaved individuals could often process and even enjoy memories of the deceased without the high emotional arousal often experienced earlier in the grieving process.

In her later years, Sanders even began to develop the notion of a sixth phase —*fulfillment*—a point at which the grieving person could look back on his or her own life in a way that integrates the earlier loss into the fabric of that life. She believed that in this phase one's life journey only made sense given the experience of loss. While the loss was neither welcomed nor anticipated, one could no longer imagine what life would be like without that loss (Doka, 2006).

Sanders was one of the first theorists to affirm that individuals had choices *within* the mourning process. Her writing emphasized that bereaved individuals were active participants in the mourning process rather than simply persons passively coping with a process where they experienced little control. Sanders's phase of renewal even presaged such current trends in contemporary bereavement theory such as grief as a transformative experience (Neimeyer, 2001; Prend, 1997; Schneider, 1994) where a loss can lead to significant personal growth as bereaved persons struggle to readapt to life without the deceased. These concepts are supported in the research of Calhoun and Tedeschi (2006) on *posttraumatic growth,* which emphasized that even a painful loss can be a source of growth.

This work accentuates the point that the goal of therapy is not to "recover" from the loss. Rather it suggests counselors pose a larger question—"How will you change in response to this loss?" Within that question is the implication that individuals can actively respond to loss. Grieving individuals need not be passive in the face of loss and grief. While they might have no choice about the death, they do retain choices about what they will do with their losses and their grief.

From relinquishing ties to revising and renewing relationships
Freud (1917) suggested that the major task in grief was to sever bonds with the deceased in order to reinvest in other relationships. By the 1980s, this notion was already under challenge (Attig, 1987; Doka, 1984). His research from the Harvard Child Bereavement Study led Worden (1991), as noted earlier, to revise his wording of his fourth task from "withdrawing emotional energy from the deceased and reinvesting in others" to "relocating the deceased" or, in the newest edition (2009), "to find an enduring connection to the deceased in the midst of embarking on a new life." In making these revisions, Worden emphasized that an ongoing relationship remained between the deceased and the survivor, albeit in a different form. This challenge found its fullest treatment in the groundbreaking book *Continuing Bonds: New Understandings of Grief* edited by Klass, Silverman, and Nickman (1996). These editors and their many contributors stress that throughout history and across cultures bereaved individuals have maintained bonds with their deceased. In short, detachment from the deceased is not normative, essential, or even desired in at least many cases. Most survivors continue to remember the deceased in many ways. Moreover, a significant deceased person is part of one's own identity and has left ongoing legacies (and perhaps liabilities) that continue to influence a survivor's behavior. Survivors retain spiritual ties such as the belief the deceased is interceding for them or that they will be reunited in an afterlife. In addition, LaGrand (1999) described another connection that he labeled "extraordinary experiences." Here survivors have dreams, experiences, and other phenomena after the death of someone they loved that seem to suggest to them a continuing presence of the deceased. Often these experiences were therapeutic—reaffirming a bond and offering comfort to the bereaved individual. Such experiences are common in bereavement. Counselors should include queries about such experiences as they assess grief reactions, as many bereaved individuals are reluctant to discuss such events even though they may be comforted by these experiences.

There are other therapeutic implications to the concept of continuing bonds. Grief counselors should reaffirm to clients that the goal of grief therapy is not to abolish memories of the deceased. The amelioration of grief means that over time the intensity of the grief experience lessens and individuals function in ways comparable to (or perhaps even better than) they did prior to the loss. As termination of a counseling relationship nears, it is helpful to suggest, and even identify, that there may be surges of grief years later that are brought on by significant life events or major transitions. However, it is important for counselors to recognize that not all connections are helpful (Stroebe, 2006). Some individuals may retain connections to the deceased that impair relationships with others or hinder adaptation to the loss.

From seeing grief as simply a normal transitional process to recognizing more complicated variants and the necessity for careful assessment

For years, the field of thanatology has eschewed a medical model of grief, avoiding terms such as "symptoms." Grief, it is argued, is a normal and natural part of the life cycle, not an illness. Grief is simply an experience that individuals encounter as they cope with inevitable transition and loss. Yet there also has been recognition that for some individuals, grief is inherently complicated (see, for example, Rando, 1993). Freud's (1917) classic paper, "Mourning and Melancholia," dealt with this very issue—trying to differentiate (somewhat unsuccessfully) between mourning, a normal response to a transitional event, and melancholia (or depression), a complicated variant. There is no category in the current *Diagnostic and Statistical Manual of Mental Disorders (DSM-IV-TR)* that expressly and directly deals with complicated variants of grief. However, there are a number of proposals before the American Psychiatric Association to add a category dealing with complicated grief to the forthcoming *DSM-5*. In addition, there is also a recommendation to remove the "bereavement exclusion" (that is, the statement in the *DSM-IV-TR* that the diagnosis of depression is excluded when the symptoms can be accounted for by bereavement from a recent loss) from the diagnostic criteria for depression. The seriousness with which these proposals have been received is a sign that there may be an increasing recognition that the stress on the normalcy of loss and grief may have led to a neglect of more problematic variants. It also may be that the growth of managed care in the United States has contributed to a desire for a clear grief-related diagnostic code.

Concurrent with this emphasis on complicated grief has been an ongoing debate on the effectiveness of grief counseling. This resulted from an early review article by Neimeyer (2000) where he suggested that unfocused interventions might do more harm than good. Larson and Hoyt (2007) strongly challenged Neimeyer's (2000) methodology and conclusions. Current thought emphasizes that grief interventions can be therapeutic if clients are genuinely in need, carefully assessed, and interventions are individually tailored (Gamino & Ritter, 2009).

This discussion suggests the need for practitioners to constantly evaluate grief therapy and other forms of interventions such as grief groups. Underlying that requirement for ongoing evaluation is a concept that as a field there needs to be more integration between clinical practice and research. This integration is facilitated when researchers and theoreticians are careful to explore the practice applications of their work, as well as when clinicians take an empirical orientation to therapy—constantly assessing how well their therapy is assisting the client's adaptation to loss.

Conclusion

Throughout the past decade and a half, understandings of grief have experienced major modifications. Future changes and challenges are likely to continue to transform the ways grief is understood. Increasing cultural diversity, demographic changes such as the aging of the baby boomers, and the rise of the Internet as a source of significant grief support and memorialization as well as a basis for cyberspace relationships, are likely to continue to challenge perspectives on loss and grief. Since grief counseling represents a core skill—central to counseling—it is essential and ethically required that counselors utilize models that are both current and evidence-based.

Editor's Note: This chapter was revised from Doka, K. J. (2007). Challenging the paradigm: New understandings of grief. In K. J. Doka (Ed.), *Living with grief: Before and after the death*, Washington, DC: Hospice Foundation of America.

Kenneth J. Doka, *PhD, MDiv, is a professor of gerontology at the Graduate School of The College of New Rochelle and senior consultant to the Hospice Foundation of America. A prolific author and editor, Dr. Doka serves as editor of HFA's* Living with Grief® *book series, its* Journeys *newsletter, and numerous other books and publications. Dr. Doka has served as a panelist on HFA's* Living with Grief® *video programs for 17 years. Dr. Doka was elected president of the Association for Death Education and Counseling (ADEC) in 1993. In 1995, he was elected to the Board of Directors of the International Work Group on*

Death, Dying, and Bereavement and served as its chair from 1997–99. ADEC presented him with an award for Outstanding Contributions in the Field of Death Education in 1998. In 2006, Dr. Doka was grandfathered in as a mental health counselor under New York's first state licensure of counselors. Dr. Doka is an ordained Lutheran minister.

REFERENCES

Attig, T. (1987). Grief, love and separation. In C. Corr and R. Pacholski (Eds.), *Death: Completion and discovery.* Lakewood, OH: The Association for Death Education and Counseling.

Bonanno, G. (2004). Loss, trauma and human resilience: Have we underestimated the human capacity to thrive after extremely aversive events? *American Psychologist, 59,* 20–28.

Boss, P. (1999). *Ambiguous loss: Learning to live with unresolved grief.* Cambridge, MA: Harvard University Press.

Bowlby, J., & Parkes, C. M. (1970). Separation and loss. In Anthony, E. J., & Koupernik, C. (Eds.), *The child in his family: Volume 1: International yearbook of child psychiatry and allied professions* (pp. 180–198). New York: John Wiley.

Bruce, E. J., & Schultz, C. L. (2001). *Nonfinite loss and grief: A psychoeducational approach.* Baltimore, MD: Paul H. Brooks Publishing Co.

Calhoun, L., & Tedeschi, R. (Eds.). (2006). *Handbook of posttraumatic growth.* Mahwah, NJ: Lawrence Erlbaum Associates.

Corr, C. A. (1992). A task-based approach to coping with dying. *Omega: Journal of Death and Dying, 24,* 81–94.

Corr, C. A., & Doka, K. J. (1994). Current models on death, dying, and bereavement. *Critical Care Nursing Clinics of North America, 6,* 545–552.

Doka, K. J. (1984). Grief. In R. Kastenbaum & B. Kastenbaum (Eds.), *Encyclopedia of death* (pp. 127–131). Phoenix, AZ: Oryx Press.

Doka, K. J. (Ed.). (1989). *Disenfranchised grief: Recognizing hidden sorrow.* Lexington, MA: Lexington Press.

Doka, K. J. (1993). The spiritual crises of bereavement. In K. J. Doka (with J. Morgan) (Ed.), *Death and spirituality* (pp. 185–195). Amityville, NY: Baywood.

Doka, K. J. (Ed.). (2002). *Disenfranchised grief: New directions, challenges, and strategies for practice.* Champaign, IL: Research Press.

Doka, K. J. (2006). Fulfillment as Sanders' sixth phase of bereavement: The unfinished work of Catherine Sanders. *Omega: Journal of Death and Dying, 52,* 141–149.

Doka, K. J. (Ed.). (2007). *Living with grief: Before and after the death.* Washington, DC: Hospice Foundation of America.

Doka, K. J. (2009). *Counseling individuals with life-threatening illness.* New York: Springer.

Doka, K. J., & Tucci, A. S. (Eds.). (2008). *Living with grief: Children and adolescents.* Washington, DC: Hospice Foundation of America.

Doka, K. J., & Martin, T. L. (2010). *Grieving beyond gender: Understanding the ways men and women mourn* (Revised Edition). New York: Routledge.

Field, D., Hockey, J., & Small, N. (Eds.). (1997). *Death, gender and ethnicity.* New York: Routledge.

Freud, S. (1957). *Mourning and melancholia.* In J. Strachey (Ed. & Trans.), *The standard edition of the complete psychological works of Sigmund Freud* (Vol. 14, pp. 273–300). London: Hogarth. (Original work published in 1917).

Garces-Foley, K. (Ed.). (2006). *Death and religion in a changing world.* Armonk, NY: M.E. Sharpe.

Gamino, L., & Ritter, R. (2009). *Ethical practice in grief counseling.* New York: Springer.

Harvey, J. (1998). *Perspectives on loss: A sourcebook.* Philadelphia, PA: Brunner/Mazel.

Holloway, K. (2002). *Passed on: African-American mourning stories.* Durham, NC: Duke University Press.

Jacobs, S., & Prigerson, H. G. (2000). Psychotherapy of traumatic grief: A review of evidence for psychotherapeutic treatments. *Death Studies, 21,* 471–498.

Klass, D., Silverman, P., & Nickman, S. (Eds.). (1996). *Continuing bonds: New understandings of grief.* Washington, DC: Taylor & Francis.

Kübler-Ross, E. (1969). *On Death and Dying.* New York: Macmillan.

LaGrand, L. (1999). *Messages and miracles: Extraordinary experiences of the bereaved.* St. Paul, MN: Llewellyn Publications.

Larson, D., & Hoyt, W. (2007). What has become of grief counseling? An evaluation of the empirical foundations of the new pessimism. *Professional Psychology: Research and Practice, 38,* 347–355.

Lindemann, E. (1944). Symptomatology and management of acute grief. *American Journal of Psychiatry, 101,* 141–148.

Maciejewski, P., Zhang, B., Block, S., & Prigerson, H. G. (2007). An empirical examination of the stage theory of grief. *JAMA: Journal of the American Medical Association, 277*(7), 716–723.

Martin, T., & Doka, K. J. (2000). *Men don't cry, women do: Transcending gender stereotypes of grief.* Philadelphia: Brunner/Mazel.

Metzger, A. M. (1979). A Q-methodological study of the Kübler-Ross stage theory. *Omega: Journal of Death and Dying, 10,* 291–302.

Neimeyer, R. A. (2000). Grief therapy and research as essential tensions: Prescriptions for a progressive partnership. *Death Studies, 24,* 603–610.

Neimeyer, R. A. (2001). *Meaning reconstruction and the meaning of loss.* Washington, DC: American Psychological Association.

Nolen-Hoeksema, S., McBride, A., & Larson, J. (1997). Rumination and psychological distress among bereaved partners. *Journal of Personality and Social Psychology, 72,* 855–862.

Parkes, C. M. (1970). The first year of bereavement: A longitudinal study of the reaction of London widows to the death of their husbands. *Psychiatry, 33,* 442–467.

Prigerson, H. G., & Maciejewski, P. (2006). A call for sound empirical testing and evaluation for complicated grief proposed for DSM-V. *Omega: Journal of Death and Dying, 52,* 9–20.

Prend, A. (1997). *Transcending loss.* New York: Berkley Books.

Puchalski, C. (2006). *A time for listening and caring: Spirituality and the care of the chronically ill and dying.* New York: Oxford University Press.

Rando, T. A. (1993). *The treatment of complicated mourning.* Champaign, IL: Research Press.

Rando, T. A. (Ed.). (2000). *Clinical dimensions of anticipatory mourning: Theory and practice in working with the dying, their loved ones, and their caregivers.* Champaign, IL: Research Press.

Roos, S. (2002). *Chronic sorrow: A living loss.* New York: Brunner-Routledge.

Rosenblatt, P. C., & Wallace, B. (2005). *African-American grief.* New York: Routledge.

Sanders, C. (1989). *Grief: The mourning after: Dealing with adult bereavement.* New York: Wiley.

Schneider, J. (1994). *Finding my way: Healing and transformation through grief and loss.* Colfax, WI: Seasons Press.

Schulz, R., & Aderman, D. (1974). Clinical research and the stages of dying. *Omega: Journal of Death and Dying, 5,* 137–144.

Silverman, P. (2000). *Never too young to know: Death in children's lives.* New York: Oxford University Press.

Stroebe, M., & Schut, H. (1999). The Dual Process Model of coping with bereavement: Rationale and description. *Death Studies, 23,* 197–224.

Stroebe, M. (April, 2006). Continuing bonds in bereavement: Toward theoretical understanding. Keynote presentation to the Association of Death Education and Counseling, Albuquerque, NM.

Sue, D. W., & Sue, D. (2008). *Counseling the culturally diverse: Theory and practice* (5th ed.). New York: John Wiley and Sons.

Worden, J. W. (1982). *Grief counseling and grief therapy: A handbook for the mental health practitioner.* New York: Springer. (2nd ed.—1991; 3rd ed.—2002; 4th ed.—2009).

Worden, J. W. (1996). *Children and grief: When a parent dies.* New York: Guilford Press.

Wortman, C., & Silver, R. (1989). The myths of coping with loss. *The Journal of Counseling and Clinical Psychology, 57,* 349–357.

Wortman, C., & Silver, R. (2001). The myths of coping with loss revisited. In M. Stroebe, R. Hansson, W. Stroebe, & H. Schut (Eds.), *Handbook of bereavement research: Consequences, coping, and care* (pp. 405–429). Washington, DC: American Psychological Association.

PART I

New Perspectives on Death and Dying

The 1969 publication of Elisabeth Kübler-Ross's *On Death and Dying* was an epochal event in thanatology. While certainly not the first publication on death and dying, it rapidly became the most well known. In many ways, the timing for such a book was right. Two years earlier, in 1967, Cicely Saunders founded St. Christopher's Hospice in London—an institution that would play a pivotal role in the worldwide development of hospice and palliative care.

Moreover, Kübler-Ross's work fit in well with the cultural themes of that time. In an era that called for natural birth, she advocated a more natural form of death. In a time that rebelled against dehumanizing technology, she modeled compassionate, patient-centered care.

Kübler-Ross was a wonderful and charismatic promoter of her work, and a tireless and engaging speaker. Kübler-Ross's Model of Five Stages was easy to assimilate and promoted a notion that one could master even this final crisis. Patients could be moved from denial to acceptance, offering a model of medical management that even shared the staging language common in the discussion of disease. Her model soon became a preeminent one in medical, nursing, and counseling education—one that moved from coping with dying, to grieving, to a variety of other crises.

Yet, it is important to recognize that over 40 years have passed since the publication of *On Death and Dying*. While Kübler-Ross's work has historical importance and heuristic value, there are more current approaches, new perspectives on dying, death, grief, and loss. This book seeks to outline those advances even as it acknowledges a debt to a pioneer.

That certainly is the point of Charles Corr's opening chapter on the strengths and limitations of Kübler-Ross's model. Corr recognizes the contributions of Kübler-Ross, especially in her call to listen to the dying patient and to heed her advocacy of compassionate care for the dying. However, Corr also notes the many methodological difficulties with her Stage Theory as well as the lack of evidence validating such an approach. To Corr, the enduring legacy of Kübler-Ross is to be found in her advocacy of both compassionate care and the development of thanatological education rather than her theory.

Corr's second chapter reviews one of the developments in our understanding of the dying process—anticipatory grief and mourning. Corr notes that the older notions of anticipatory grief often mistakenly focused on the belief that grieving an anticipated loss now would make subsequent adjustment easier after the death. As Corr recognizes, that notion is now discredited. Instead, we understand that anticipatory grief and mourning are distinct processes; one reacts and adjusts not to a future loss but rather all the losses—present and future—experienced within the illness.

Kenneth Doka's chapter finishes this section. Here Doka reviews more current models of the dying process—ones based on a notion of tasks rather than stages. Such an approach focuses on the common issues that individuals and families face as they adapt to life-threatening illness rather than posits common reactions. Doka suggests that the complexity of such task models may be a factor inhibiting their use.

Certainly Stage Models are ingrained within the popular imagination—references to them appear in television shows and movies, and they also remain prevalent in health education. This raises one final question. How should one respond to persons, especially supervisors, still tied to older models? Certainly we hope that this book may offer education on newer approaches. It is an ethical mandate to work from the most current knowledge. After all, would a cancer patient wish to be treated by an oncologist steeped in the approaches offered in 1969?

CHAPTER 1

Strengths and Limitations of the Stage Theory Proposed by Elisabeth Kübler-Ross

Charles A. Corr

Elisabeth Kübler-Ross

In 1969, Elisabeth Kübler-Ross (1926–2004) published *On Death and Dying*. The book became an international best seller, led to worldwide fame, and set off countless requests for its author to give interviews, lectures, and seminars on subjects that soon became the main focus of her professional life. In her writings and speaking engagements, Kübler-Ross expressed views on many subjects including the afterlife, spiritual guides, out-of-body experiences, and near-death experiences, but she is best known for her theory of five stages of dying.

It may help to note that Kübler-Ross described herself as stubborn, opinionated, independent, and unconventional (Gill, 1980; Kübler-Ross, 1997). As a young person growing up in Switzerland, she was determined to become a doctor despite her father's wishes and a childhood experience of hospitalization in which she was isolated and separated from her family by what she viewed as an impersonal and uncaring system. After qualifying as a physician, Elisabeth Kübler married a fellow medical student from America (Emanuel Ross). The couple moved to the United States, and she accepted a residency in psychiatry because becoming pregnant had disqualified her from her preferred field of pediatrics.

In the fall of 1965, Kübler-Ross was a new faculty member at the University of Chicago Billings Hospital when four theology students asked her to help them understand death as the biggest crisis in life. She offered to identify dying patients with whom to conduct interviews, but many other physicians at the hospital were skeptical about her goals. Several expressed concerns about exploiting vulnerable patients and were unwilling to grant access to their patients. As she wrote, "It suddenly seemed that there were no dying patients in this huge hospital" (1969, p. 23). Nevertheless, Kübler-Ross soon found herself leading an unorthodox but popular weekly seminar in which she would interview a patient with one-way glass separating him or her from students, then leading a discussion with the students after the patient had left. It was this seminar that led to her book and the theory it advanced.

THE FIVE STAGES

The Stage Theory of dying arose from interviews over a period of approximately two-and-a-half years that Kübler-Ross conducted with some 200 adult patients who were living with a terminal illness. Each of the stages can be associated with a typical expression.

Stage	*Typical Expression*
First Stage: Denial	"No it's not true, no, it cannot involve me!"
Second Stage: Anger	"Why me?"
Third Stage: Bargaining	"Yes me, but . . ."

Fourth Stage: Depression
   Reactive
   Preparatory
	Responding to past and present losses
	Anticipating and responding to losses yet to come

Fifth Stage: Acceptance	Described as a stage "almost void of feelings"

Each stage of this model represents a typical human reaction:
- Denial involves a reaction to the shock of the diagnosis; it reflects unwillingness to acknowledge the fact that one is dying or outright rejection of that fact. Denial is also a kind of buffer or protective barrier aimed at holding off the implications of terminal illness.
- Anger arises when denial can no longer be sustained; anger, rage, envy, and resentment at least partially acknowledge that the individual is dying but also acknowledge that this is not fair or right. Anger can be seen as a retort to the psychological pain generated by the diagnosis; anger is often displaced and projected outward, fairly or not, toward care providers, God, or other perceived contributors to the situation.
- Bargaining involves some degree of resignation to what cannot be controlled, combined with efforts to gain some degree of influence

by focusing (realistically or unrealistically) on what might be done to postpone the inevitable or arrange for that outcome to occur in ways perceived as more tolerable by the individual. In return, bargaining offers pledges of various types to God or the doctors, although Kübler-Ross was clear that most individuals would not and should not be expected to keep these promises.
- Depression reflects increasing misery as the realities of the situation gradually set in; as such, depression focuses on the individual's great sense of loss, either on past and present losses in the form of reactive depression, or on future, anticipated losses such as the expected loss of all love objects in the form of preparatory depression.
- Acceptance is described as "the final stage when the end is more promising or there is not enough strength left to live" (1969, p. 176); different individuals may experience acceptance in different ways, ranging from looking forward to impending death as an end to a protracted process, a relief from suffering, or an opening to an afterlife, to grudging acknowledgment of one's fate.

One important aspect of this theory that has often been overlooked is the author's insistence that "The one thing that usually persists through all these stages is hope" (1969, p. 138). Kübler-Ross stressed to care providers the importance of not undercutting hope, of allowing dying persons to keep up their hope so that it "should always be maintained whether we can agree with the form or not" (1969, p. 265).

Why Did This Theory Gain Such Rapid and Widespread Popularity?

The basic answer seems to be that it was simple, easy to understand, and touched chords in many who agreed with Kübler-Ross that much care of dying persons had taken on qualities of depersonalization and dehumanization. People agreed with Kübler-Ross when she argued that prevailing attitudes of care providers and healthcare systems often contributed to the loneliness and misery felt by many dying persons. Kübler-Ross concluded that "for the patient death itself is not the problem but dying is feared because of the accompanying sense of hopelessness, helplessness, and isolation" (1969, p. 268). Her words were acknowledged by many, including one British woman who, on the basis of her experiences in *Living with a Man Who Is Dying* (Evans, 1971, p. 83), wrote, "We have created systems which protect us in the aggregate from facing up to the very things that as individuals we most need to know."

The late 1960s and 1970s were a time when many caregivers and scholars began to wonder whether care provided to those who were dying was properly recognizing and responding to those persons' needs (e.g., Hinton, 1963; LeShan, 1964; Mount, Jones, & Patterson, 1974; Rees, 1972). It was also the time when Dr. Cicely Saunders founded St. Christopher's Hospice in southeast London in 1967, an institution that inspired the modern hospice movement and came to demonstrate what that form of care could achieve (DuBoulay, 1984; see also Parkes, 2007).

Looking back on developments since that time, especially the rapid growth of the modern hospice movement around the world, it is now clear that our distorted understandings of the needs of the dying did not serve those vulnerable individuals very well. It is equally evident that efforts to protect society by distancing communities from these individual members also did not serve very well the needs of the larger community that needed to appreciate the realities of dying, death, and bereavement as important parts of human life.

Many people accepted the invitation that Kübler-Ross extended to try to imagine themselves in the position of dying patients so as to understand and tolerate the reactions of those individuals rather than judging them. This openness to the point of view that Kübler-Ross advocated was found in both healthcare professionals (particularly nurses, who were among her most eager students) and ordinary lay persons. It was especially supported by those who had been close to dying family members and by some healthcare professionals who were amazed by how the very systems in which they had worked treated them when they found themselves to be dying.

In terms of the theory's simplicity, Kübler-Ross wrote, "I am simply telling the stories of my patients who shared their agonies, their expectations, and their frustrations with us" (1969, p. xi). That comment is humble and attractive, but it is also a bit disingenuous. No one simply tells the stories of others. As we choose which stories to tell and how to tell them, all of us select and interpret in some degree or other whatever it is that we relate.

In fact, Kübler-Ross construed the stories she described in terms of the theoretical framework she developed. And she described her five "stages" in various ways, for example, as "reactions," "defenses," "defense mechanisms," "coping mechanisms," and "adaptations." Thus, she began chapter VIII in her book in the following way:

> We have discussed so far the different stages that people go through when they are faced with tragic news—defense mechanisms in psychiatric terms, coping mechanisms to deal with extremely difficult situations. These means will last for different periods of time and will replace each other or exist at times side by side. (1969, p. 138)

In other words, Kübler-Ross depicted her theory as a general model or way of categorizing experiences many individuals have when facing awareness of their own finality. In short, the five stages represent a typology of some prominent psychosocial reactions to experiences that may be associated with dying.

Kübler-Ross wrote in ways that leave a degree of ambiguity as to whether she believed only some or all dying persons actually do, will, or must go through her five stages. For example, at one point she wrote: "If a patient has had enough time (i.e., not a sudden, unexpected death) and has been given some help in working through the previously described stages, he will reach a stage during which he is neither depressed nor angry about his 'fate'" (1969, p. 112). Here, the key word "will" contrasts with "can" in another passage in which Kübler-Ross wrote about "patients who are fortunate enough to have time to work through some of their conflicts while they are sick and who can come to a deeper understanding and perhaps appreciation of the things they still have to enjoy" (1969, p. 273). And elsewhere she offered the following observation: "Simple people with less education, sophistication, social ties, and professional obligations seem in general to have somewhat less difficulty in facing this final crisis than people of affluence who lose a great deal more in terms of material luxuries, comfort, and number of interpersonal relationships" (1969, p. 265).

Kübler-Ross also argued that the types of reactions described in her stage-based theory are not confined solely to dying persons. Thus, she wrote that "Family members undergo different stages of adjustment similar to the ones described for our patients" (1969, p. 168). Indeed, as important components of the human experience, these reactions may be experienced by anyone who enters into the experiential world of those who are dying, including care providers. And because common reactions like denial or anger are familiar features of many everyday experiences, they are not limited to end-of-life situations. As such, it was easy for readers to identify with the many vignettes and concrete examples that fill the pages of *On Death and Dying*.

In addition, Kübler-Ross described the five stages in her theory in broad terms. For example, "denial" and "acceptance" are essentially presented as opposites on a continuum. Although the other three stages—anger, bargaining, and depression—may vary in intensity, character, and focus, they appear mainly as transitional factors experienced in the process of moving from denial to acceptance. Denial and acceptance are themselves each formulated in ways that allow them to apply to a spectrum of reactions: from a complete rejection of one's status as a seriously-ill person, to an unwillingness to admit one is dying or that death is more or less imminent, on the one hand; and from acknowledgment, resignation, and acquiescence to welcoming, on the other hand.

According to Kübler-Ross, "Denial, at least partial denial, is used by almost all patients, not only during the first stages of illness or following confrontation, but also later on from time to time" (1969, p. 39). She added that denial is "a healthy way of dealing with the uncomfortable and painful situation with which some of these patients have to live for a long time. Denial functions as a buffer after unexpected shocking news, allows the patient to collect himself and, with time, mobilize other, less radical defenses" (1969, p. 39).

CRITICISMS OF THE STAGE THEORY OF DYING

Despite the way in which this Stage Theory of dying captured popular and professional attention in many circles, it has faced a series of serious criticisms. One of the most detailed evaluations of this stage-based model raised the following points: (1) the existence of these stages as such has not been demonstrated; (2) no evidence has been presented that people actually do move from Stage 1 through Stage 5; (3) the limitations of the method have not been acknowledged; (4) the line is blurred between description and prescription; (5) the totality of the person's life is neglected in favor of the supposed stages of dying; and (6) the resources, pressures, and characteristics of the immediate environment, which can make a tremendous difference, are not taken into account (Kastenbaum, 2009). In addition, Kübler-Ross's theory assumes or at least suggests that we can describe the way in which all persons respond to the stress of dying, independently of any social or cultural influences. But in fact, our social and cultural environments are essential variables that affect how we respond to stress.

More specifically, there are at least three broad types of criticisms that have been leveled against this Stage Theory of dying. First, scientific research has not corroborated the model. Kübler-Ross herself offered nothing beyond the authority of her own clinical impressions and illustrations from selected examples to sustain her theory. She advanced no further empirical evidence to support or confirm the accuracy, soundness, or efficacy of the model. Nor did she attend to the fact that this theory had its origin in one author's clinical impressions drawn from a particular social population dying in particular ways and in a particular time and location. Instead, she simply continued to assume that these stages were obviously authoritative. In short, there has been no independent confirmation of the validity or reliability of the theory. In addition, the early empirical research from the 1970s did not confirm this model (Metzger, 1979; Schulz & Aderman, 1974). And Kübler-Ross herself applied this theory to children and others in ways not warranted by its original origin in interviews with specific groups of dying adults.

Second, the five sets of psychosocial reactions at the heart of the theory can be criticized as overly broad in their formulation, insufficient to reflect the full range of human reactions to death and dying, and inadequately grounded for the wide-ranging ways in which they have been used (Corr, 1993). The expansive way in which these five reactions are formulated has already been noted. Of course, Kübler-Ross did not invent these five reaction patterns; her inspiration was to apply them individually to the human experiences of dying and facing death, and to link them together as part of a larger theoretical schema. Framing her theory in terms of "defensive reactions," however, was not necessarily helpful because as Weisman (1984, p. 36) has observed, coping "is positive in approach; defending is negative."

The trait of "depression" seems particularly curious as an element in a healthy, normative process of reacting to dying—unless it really means "sadness"—since clinical depression is a psychiatric diagnosis of illness. Moreover, we need not believe there are only five ways in which to react to dying and death any more than that there are only five ways in which to react to life and living.

Third, the theory has been criticized for linking the five reaction patterns together as stages in a larger process. In part, Kübler-Ross seems to have agreed with this point since she argued for fluidity, give-and-take, the possibility of experiencing more than one of these reactions simultaneously, and an ability to jump around from one "stage" to another. As she wrote, "these stages do not replace each other but can exist next to each other and overlap at times" (1969, p. 263). If so, this is not really a theory of stages, which would involve a linear progression and regression like steps on a ladder or calibrations on a thermometer. In short, the language of "stages" seems inappropriate for what essentially are a cluster of different psychodynamic reactions to a particular type of life experience.

This last point is important because some have shifted the emphasis of the theory from description (recounting how some people actually do react to impending death) to prescription (asserting how people should or ought to react to impending death). Some practitioners have been reported to tell dying persons they have already experienced one of the five stages and should now "move on" to another, while others have complained about individuals whom they view as "stuck" in the dying process. When coupled with the limits imposed by only five general categories of reaction to dying, this tends to suppress the individuality of dying persons (and others) by coercing them into a rigid, preestablished framework in which they are expected to live out an agenda at the end of life that is imposed on them by others. Perhaps that is why one person with a life-threatening illness complained that "Being invisible I invite only generalizations" (Rosenthal, 1973, p. 39).

In fact, no one has to die in any particular way. To believe otherwise is to attempt to impose one's own convictions on vulnerable people who are coping with dying; it is the exact opposite of allowing individuals to sing their own songs near or at the end of their lives.

Concerns about misuse of this stage-based theory are particularly ironic since Kübler-Ross set out to argue that dying persons are mistreated when they are objectified and dealt with in stereotypical ways. As Kübler-Ross herself wrote, "I repeat my conviction that a patient has a right to die in peace and dignity. He should not be used to fulfill our own needs when his own wishes are in opposition to ours" (1969, p. 177). As a result, what seems to be widespread acclaim for this theory in popular culture and in certain forms of professional education (e.g., Downe-Wamboldt & Tamlyn, 1997; Friedman & James, 2008) contrasts with sharp criticism presented more than 30 years ago by scholars and practitioners who work most closely with dying persons (e.g., Feigenberg, 1980; Pattison, 1977; Shneidman, 1980/1995; Weisman, 1977). That suggests there may be some justification for the argument that this stage-based model for coping with dying has been widely accepted for reasons other than its own intrinsic strengths (Klass, 1982; Klass & Hutch, 1985).

Kübler-Ross did not respond to any of the scholarly criticisms or comments and was perhaps not even aware of them. Although she did not offer additional evidence or arguments to support her stage-based theory of coping with dying, she continued to assert the five stages in nearly all of her writings and presentations that followed *On Death and Dying*. In fact, in a book published just a year after her death, Kübler-Ross and David Kessler (2005) applied this same theory to post-death bereavement experiences. The very subtitle of this book—*Finding the Meaning of Grief through the Five Stages of Loss*—is clearly meant to re-affirm the well-known stage-based theory while at the same time expanding it from a focus on dying to all types of loss. Although there is no obvious or empirical justification for undertaking such an expansion, what the authors have to say about these stages is illuminating:

> The stages have evolved since their introduction, and they have been very misunderstood over the past three decades.... They are responses to loss that many people have, but there is not a typical response to loss, as there is no typical loss. Our grief is as individual as our lives.
>
> The five stages... are tools to help us frame and identify what we may be feeling. But they are not stops on some linear timeline in grief. Not everyone goes through all of them or goes in a prescribed order. (p. 7)

LESSONS FROM THE STAGE THEORY OF DYING

Despite these criticisms, there are several positive things to say about the model proposed by Kübler-Ross. Above all, this model helps normalize and humanize the experiences of dying persons by demonstrating that dying is a human process, not merely a series of biological events. It also draws attention to challenges encountered by dying persons and to their needs as living human beings. The theory became readily accepted within the popular culture perhaps because it describes reactions to a difficult situation in ways people can easily understand, and seemingly provides a tool to help dying persons. The model also allows others to contemplate their own reactions when interacting with a dying person. In addition, the theory argues against the view that only mentally deranged or suicidal persons could truly accept their deaths.

In all of this, Kübler-Ross was an early and important contributor to the death awareness movement. She was, in the best sense of the terms, a publicist or propagandist for dying persons and their family members, advocating for improvements in the care they needed. As such, she helped to establish the atmosphere in which the modern hospice movement developed, although her ideas did not emerge from within that movement. She did not involve herself in any great degree in such basic features of the hospice philosophy as an emphasis on holistic care, an effort to provide good physical care and relief from distressing symptoms of disease, and the indispensability of interdisciplinary teamwork.

Three important lessons can be learned from this Stage Theory of dying. Interestingly enough, each of these lessons can be found, at least implicitly, in the short preface to *On Death and Dying*. The first lesson is that those who are coping with dying are still alive and often have what Kübler-Ross called "unfinished needs" they may want to address. This is fundamental and paramount. Dying patients are living human beings, and coping with dying is a humane and vital process. As his wife, Linda, says of her husband, Willie Loman, in the play, *Death of a Salesman*, "He's a human being, and a terrible thing is happening to him. So attention must be paid" (Miller, 1948, p. 40). This is the lesson about all who are dying and about all who are coping with dying, whether they themselves are actually dying at the moment. Each of these individuals will react in their own particular ways to the death-related challenges that confront them and may have their own needs to address.

The second lesson is that others cannot be or become effective providers of care unless they listen actively to those who cope with dying and work with them to identify their needs and psychosocial processes. This is so basic as to be almost obvious, if one did not know that it is practiced far less frequently than it is preached. How can one ever presume to care for another human being if one does not actively listen to the needs and priorities of that person? How can one be an effective care provider if one is content to act on the basis of stereotypes or generalizations? How can one dare to approach another human being as a provider of care without entering into a relationship with that person within which he or she plays at least a part (if not the main role) in defining his or her own coping tasks? This is a lesson about becoming and being a provider of care.

The third lesson is that we all need to learn from those who are dying and coping with dying in order to know ourselves better as limited, vulnerable, finite, and mortal, but also as resilient, adaptable, interdependent, and worthy of love. Here, the advice is to draw upon the experiences of those who are coping with dying for our own benefit and instruction. Kübler-Ross would rightly have us regard dying persons and those who are coping with dying as our teachers. This is reminiscent of Socrates, who constantly asked those whom he encountered to examine their own lives and to teach him about the subjects they discussed, who suggested that true wisdom is little more than a preparation for death, and who regarded the role of teacher as one of assisting others to draw out of themselves their full potential for living. This is a lesson for all of us.

The language and the interpretations of the three lessons described here are my own. Kübler-Ross put these lessons in the following way when she wrote that her book:

> is not meant to be a textbook on how to manage dying patients, nor is it intended as a complete study of the psychology of dying. It is simply an account of a new and challenging opportunity to refocus on the patient as a human being, to include him in dialogues, to learn from him the strengths and weaknesses of our hospital management of the patient. We have asked him to be our teacher so that we may learn more about the final stages of life with all its anxieties, fears, and hopes. (1969, p. xi)

Concluding Thoughts

Elisabeth Kübler-Ross was a pioneering author and educator who contributed in important ways to the development of our understandings of coping with dying. She deserves credit for that and we should honor her for those positive contributions. We do not honor her if we settle for merely repeating the five stages, often based on little more than a superficial reading of *On Death and Dying* or, perhaps worse yet, a reliance on second-hand accounts of its theoretical content. Stages are too rigid, too linear, and, above all, too passive a metaphor for the rich, supple, and active processes that are involved in coping with dying. The goal for all those who are coping with dying is not merely to "get through" from one stage to another, to move from the presumed "unrealistic" attitude of denial to the "more realistic" attitude of acceptance. Instead, the true goal is to live as well as we can in accordance with our individual definitions of what constitutes quality in living during this often highly pressured but always very precious time in life—and to help others to do so when and as best we can.

Like any important theorist who preceded us, Elisabeth Kübler-Ross helped advance our thinking in this field and sparked important efforts to find good in those who are coping with dying and in ourselves. She offered us constructive lessons; it is our responsibility to appreciate both the strengths and the limitations of what she wrote. That will not be accomplished by merely freezing our understandings of her work in an often simplistic reading of a theoretical model set forth in 1969. Turning to the future, we have opportunities to move forward in our thinking about coping with dying and helping those who are coping with dying. Some efforts have been made in that direction (e.g., Corr, 1992; Corr, Doka, & Kastenbaum, 1999; Kastenbaum & Thuell, 1995), but we have a long way to go before we can ever hope to claim that we have a comprehensive theory of coping with dying.

Charles A. Corr, PhD, *is vice-chair of the Board of Directors of the Suncoast Institute (an affiliate of Suncoast Hospice). He is a member of the ChiPPS (Children's Project on Palliative/Hospice Services) Communications Work Group of the National Hospice and Palliative Care Organization; the Executive Committee of the National Donor Family Council; the Association for Death Education and Counseling; and the International Work Group on Death, Dying, and Bereavement (Chairperson, 1989–93). He is also professor emeritus, Southern Illinois University Edwardsville. Dr. Corr's publications in the field of death, dying, and bereavement include three dozen books and booklets, along with more than 110 chapters and articles in professional publications. His next book, the seventh edition of* Death and Dying, Life and Living *(Belmont, CA: Wadsworth), co-authored with Donna M. Corr, will be published in January 2012.*

REFERENCES

Corr, C. A. (1992). A task-based approach to coping with dying. *Omega: Journal of Death and Dying, 24,* 81–94.

Corr, C. A. (1993). Coping with dying: Lessons that we should and should not learn from the work of Elisabeth Kübler-Ross. *Death Studies, 17,* 69–83.

Corr, C. A., Doka, K. J., & Kastenbaum, R. J. (1999). Dying and its interpreters: A review of selected literature and some comments on the state of the field. *Omega: Journal of Death and Dying, 39,* 239–259.

Downe-Wamboldt, B., & Tamlyn, D. (1997). An international survey of death education trends in faculties of nursing and medicine. *Death Studies, 21,* 177–188.

DuBoulay, S. (1984). *Cicely Saunders: The founder of the modern hospice movement.* London: Hodder & Stoughton.

Evans, J. (1971). *Living with a man who is dying.* New York: Taplinger.

Feigenberg, L. (1980). *Terminal care: Friendship contracts with dying cancer patients.* New York: Brunner/Mazel.

Friedman, R., & James, J. W. (2008). The myth of the stages of dying, death and grief. *Skeptic, 14*(2). Retrieved from www.skeptic.com on October 3, 2008.

Gill, D. L. (1980). *Quest: The life of Elisabeth Kübler-Ross.* New York: Harper & Row.

Hinton, J. (1963). The physical and mental distress of the dying. *Quarterly Journal of Medicine, New Series, 32,* 1–21.

Kastenbaum, R. (2009). *Death, society, and human experience* (10th ed.). Boston: Allyn & Bacon.

Kastenbaum, R., & Thuell, S. (1995). Cookies baking, coffee brewing: Toward a contextual theory of dying. *Omega: Journal of Death and Dying, 31,* 175–187.

Klass, D. (1982). Elisabeth Kübler-Ross and the tradition of the private sphere: An analysis of symbols. *Omega: Journal of Death and Dying, 12,* 241–261.

Klass, D., & Hutch, R. A. (1985). Elisabeth Kübler-Ross as a religious leader. *Omega: Journal of Death and Dying, 16,* 89–109.

Kübler-Ross, E. (1969). *On death and dying.* New York: Macmillan.

Kübler-Ross, E. (1997). *The wheel of life: A memoir of living and dying.* New York: Scribner.

Kübler-Ross, E., & Kessler, D. (2005). *On grief and grieving: Finding the meaning of grief through the five stages of loss.* New York: Scribner.

LeShan, L. (1964). The world of the patient in severe pain of long duration. *Journal of Chronic Diseases, 17,* 119–126.

Metzger, A. M. (1979). A Q-methodological study of the Kübler-Ross stage theory. *Omega: Journal of Death and Dying, 10,* 291–302.

Miller, A. (1948). *Death of a salesman.* New York: Dramatists Play Service.

Mount, B. M., Jones, A., & Patterson, A. (1974). Death and dying: Attitudes in a teaching hospital. *Urology, 4,* 741–747.

Parkes, C. M. (Ed.). (2007). "Hospice heritage": In memory of Dame Cicely Saunders [Special issue]. *Omega: Journal of Death and Dying, 52*(1).

Pattison, E. M. (1977). *The experience of dying.* Englewood Cliffs, NJ: Prentice-Hall.

Rees, W. D. (1972). The distress of dying. *British Medical Journal, 2,* 105–107.

Rosenthal, T. (1973). *How could I not be among you?* New York: George Braziller.

Schulz, R., & Aderman, D. (1974). Clinical research and the stages of dying. *Omega: Journal of Death and Dying, 5,* 137–144.

Shneidman, E. (1980/1995). *Voices of death.* New York: Harper & Row/ Kodansha International.

Weisman, A. (1977). The psychiatrist and the inexorable. In H. Feifel (Ed.), *New meanings of death* (pp. 107–122). New York: McGraw-Hill.

Weisman, A. (1984). *The coping capacity: On the nature of being mortal.* New York: Human Sciences Press.

CHAPTER 2

Anticipatory Grief and Mourning

Charles A. Corr

HISTORICAL BACKGROUND

Credit for first drawing explicit attention to the concept of anticipatory grief is usually given to Erich Lindemann (1944). Since that time, many writers and researchers have addressed this topic, focusing on diverse groups such as dying adults, terminally ill children, their parents, and bereaved spouses (e.g., Aldrich, 1963; Siegel & Weinstein, 1983; Sourkes, 1996). In particular, Fulton and colleagues (Fulton & Fulton, 1971, 1972; Fulton & Gottesman, 1980) attempted to clarify the meaning of the phrase "anticipatory grief" and put an end to erroneous assumptions that misled many researchers. Much of this early work is reflected in books edited by Schoenberg, Carr, Kutscher, Peretz, & Goldberg (1974) and by Rando (1986), as well as in Rando's (2000b) insightful review of the literature.

While many writers have used the phrases "anticipatory grief" and "anticipatory mourning" interchangeably, Futterman, Hoffman, and Sabshin (1972) appear to have been the first to distinguish them formally, at least insofar as they viewed grief and grieving as distinct components of the mourning process. Rando (1988) conceded that the phrase "anticipatory grief" is a misnomer (for reasons explained below) but insisted that the phenomenon is a reality. In a second edited book on the subject, Rando (2000a) preferred "anticipatory mourning" as the master concept. Subsequently, Fulton (2003, p. 348) observed, "I have serious reservations regarding the heuristic value—either theoretical or practical—of the concepts 'anticipatory grief' and 'anticipatory mourning.'"

OBJECTIVES OF THIS CHAPTER

This chapter examines the distinction between anticipatory grief and anticipatory mourning, as well as the meaning of the two phrases. It describes some unhelpful assumptions that have clouded understanding of the two concepts and proposes more constructive ways of thinking about them. The immediate objectives of this chapter are (1) to help people who are experiencing anticipatory grief and mourning better understand their own reactions and responses in the face of expected losses, and (2) to enable those providing care to function more effectively in their roles. The overall goal is to demonstrate the practical value of anticipatory grief and anticipatory mourning, and provide some guidelines for helping those who are experiencing anticipatory grief and mourning.

Three Examples of Anticipatory Grief and Mourning

We can clarify experiences of anticipatory grief and anticipatory mourning through three examples: a historical report and two composite cases.

Edgar Allan Poe

In a letter dated January 4, 1848, Edgar Allan Poe wrote about repeated episodes in which his wife ruptured blood vessels while singing. Apparently, Virginia Poe suffered from an advanced case of "consumption" or what is now called tuberculosis, a case so extreme that when she engaged in what for most healthy persons would have been a benign activity she bled from her lungs.

Whenever this happened, his wife's bleeding led Poe to anticipate her death. Her loss seemed so likely, Poe writes, that "Her life was despaired of" and he "took leave of her forever" or gave her up for dead. Expecting her to die, Poe "underwent all the agonies of her death." That is, he experienced anticipatory grief in his reaction to the expected loss of his wife. His reactions were so extreme that he "became insane," only to renew his desperate love for her each time she recovered. In his periods of intense grief, Poe turned to alcohol. His drinking, he explains, was the consequence of his grief, depression, and "insanity," not the other way around. This is a familiar way of trying to manage loss and grief, although not one most counselors would recommend. What was most difficult to bear, Poe writes, was "the horrible never-ending oscillation between hope & despair which I could not longer have endured without the total loss of reason." Paradoxically, it was only upon the actual death of his wife that Poe experienced "a permanent cure." His grief and mourning did not cease, but they altered in character. Freed from the anticipation of his wife's death and from the conflicting strains of her relapses and recoveries, Poe was now able to confront the finality of her death. This meant the loss of his precious wife and his previous mode of existence, and the beginning of a new and very melancholy mode of living.

> **Extract From a Letter by Edgar Allan Poe of January 4, 1848**
>
> You say—"Can you *hint* to me what was the terrible evil which caused the irregularities so profoundly lamented?" Yes; I can do more than hint. This "evil" was the greatest which can befall a man. Six years ago, a wife, whom I loved as no man ever loved before, ruptured a blood-vessel in singing. Her life was despaired of. I took leave of her forever & underwent all the agonies of her death. She recovered partially and I again hoped. At the end of a year the vessel broke again—I went through precisely the same scene. Again in about a year afterward. Then again—again—again & even once again at varying intervals. Each time I felt all the agonies of her death—and at each accession of the disorder I loved her more dearly & clung to her life with more desperate pertinacity. But I am constitutionally sensitive—nervous in a very unusual degree. I became insane, with long intervals of horrible sanity. During these fits of absolute unconsciousness I drank, God only knows how often or how much. As a matter of course, my enemies referred the insanity to the drink rather than the drink to the insanity. I had indeed, nearly abandoned all hope of a permanent cure when I found one in the death of my wife. This I can & do endure as becomes a man—it was the horrible never-ending oscillation between hope & despair which I could not longer have endured without the total loss of reason. In the death of what was my life, then, I receive a new but—oh God! how melancholy an existence.
>
> Source: *The Letters of Edgar Allan Poe*, 1948, vol. 2, p. 356.

A Wife With a Life-Threatening Illness

Throughout their marriage, Joan and Ned Wagner had experienced no serious health problems. So they found it difficult to believe when the specialist told Joan she had a life-threatening illness and did not fully understand the gravity of the situation until they talked with their family doctor. As time passed, Joan grew progressively weaker and less able to engage in former activities. She quit her job, eventually withdrew to her bed, and gradually required increasing care. Ned took a leave from work, arranged for a visiting nurse service, and tried to help as much as he could. He told one of the nurses that he had always expected to die before Joan. Now he didn't know quite what to do.

When Joan and Ned looked to the future they realized that Joan did not have long to live and agreed to use their remaining time together as best they could. She chose to enter a hospice home care program and encouraged each of their children and grandchildren to visit and pray with them. They reviewed their financial situation, made funeral and burial plans, and put things in order as much as possible for Ned's future life as a widower.

They were able to anticipate some losses, while others occurred unexpectedly and surprised them. The hospice staff helped Joan and Ned by validating their grief reactions and offering support to each of them, by teaching them what they might expect as Joan's illness progressed, and by promising to be available whenever they were needed, both before and after Joan's death.

Joan and Ned kept a journal throughout her illness. Reading back through earlier entries they were able to see how things had changed over time. At any given point, they could identify the losses they had already experienced, those they were currently undergoing, and—most difficult—those they would soon experience, in particular the loss they both dreaded: Joan's death. As time passed, expected or anticipated losses were realized and became part of the present and then the past in this life story. Their journal recorded many losses and new challenges, many everyday incidents, and some surprises and cherished events. It was a precious time, one they tried to make as rich and meaningful as they could, a reflection of their deep love for each other.

After Joan's death, Ned told the hospice bereavement coordinator that he was surprised by the freshness and depth of his grief. He said, "We knew Joan was dying and gradually coming close to the end. We experienced a lot of grief during that time and we appreciated that you helped us engage in some constructive mourning processes. So we thought that when the moment of Joan's death would finally arrive, we would be well prepared for her loss. In fact, it almost seemed as if our grief increased. Well, perhaps that's not exactly right. What happened was that we encountered a new wave of grief. All of us, the children and I, cried and sobbed. It was almost as if we hadn't known she would die. But we did. And I guess we weren't finished with our grief by a long shot."

A Child With a Life-Threatening Illness

When Carol and Joe Sullivan were told their youngest child, Julie, had been diagnosed with a life-threatening illness, they were thunderstruck. It was all they could do to keep themselves together while they drove home and when they were with their two older children.

For Carol, the first weeks after the diagnosis were a time of intense pain and sadness. "It was a defining time in my life," she said later. "Things were never the same afterwards." Carol made an effort not to cry in front of the children but did so often when she was alone. She tried to turn to Joe to share her grief, but found he was focused almost entirely on looking up more information about Julie's disease, seeking out second opinions, and investigating alternative therapies and other interventions that might lead to a cure. He urged Carol not to give up hope and refused to believe that Julie would die almost up to the moment of her death. Unfortunately, some of the interventions he wanted to try would have inflicted harsh side effects on Julie. Carol cooperated with Joe's ideas at first, but gradually realized that Julie didn't want such severe treatment. Unlike Joe, Carol came to acknowledge that Julie would die. As a result, she concentrated on improving the quality of Julie's life, spending time with her children, and creating memories they could all look back on after Julie's death.

The hospice social worker congratulated Carol on her realistic outlook and her ability to tolerate Joe's need to deny Julie's impending death without allowing a major rift to come between them. Carol explained that her priorities were to help Julie feel safe and happy as long as she was with them, and to make it possible for every member of her family to go on after Julie's death. She said, however, that Joe was having a difficult time coping with his daughter's death.

GRIEF AND MOURNING

Grief is often described as "the emotional reaction to loss." It is that, but it is more than that. Part of the problem is that the word "emotion," as Elias (1991) pointed out, can refer either to feelings alone or to a combination of feelings, behaviors, and physical components. When people experience a major loss, such as the death of someone they love, they may react to the loss not just in how they feel but in all the dimensions of their being. Their grief often includes physical, behavioral, social, psychological (cognitive and affective), and spiritual reactions. Bereaved persons typically resent the idea that their grief should be limited to feelings alone. Even well-meaning friends frequently underestimate the depth and breadth of a person's grief by suggesting that it can simply or easily be set aside.

The example of Edgar Allan Poe demonstrates an extreme set of anticipatory grief reactions. The possibility of his wife's death became so real to him on more than one occasion that, as he wrote, he "became insane." Her impending loss reached deep into his being and caused him great agony.

By contrast, family members and care providers may assume that a person who does not express grief publicly in recognized ways (e.g., by crying) is not aware of the significance of an anticipated or actual loss. The person may be assumed not to be "dealing with" the death when, in fact, that is not correct. How grief is experienced and expressed is very much an individual matter and is influenced by social and cultural norms.

"Mourning" refers to what one does with one's grief or, more precisely, the effortful responses one makes to manage grief. Trying to cope with loss is both an individual task and one that normally is aided by social support and community rituals. When the loss, grief, and bereavement are disenfranchised, as Doka (1989, 2002) has shown, opportunities are closed off for open acknowledgment, public mourning, and receiving social support as a bereaved person. One problem with anticipatory mourning is that while well-recognized forms of social ritual are designed to help bereaved persons after a death, this kind of support is typically not available before a death. People may develop their own informal rituals to support anticipatory mourning. Some ethnic and religious groups have rituals connected with caring for the dying, and hospice programs often encourage life review and funeral planning as part of coping with an expected death. However, family members may find few ways to receive social support when they are anticipating a loss through death.

Grieving persons are often told, "Be strong," "Put a smile on your face," or "Don't dwell on bad feelings." Advice of this type is meant to urge grievers to manage or cope with their losses and grief reactions in certain socially approved ways. Such advice may serve the needs of those around the grieving person but may not be useful for the mourner. Rather, the grieving person needs to engage in constructive mourning responses in the form of tasks and processes to help cope with or try to manage his or her grief reactions and begin to develop ways of living in a world that has been changed by a current or impending loss.

Unfortunately, Edgar Allan Poe sought to cope with the anticipated loss of his wife and with his extreme grief reactions by turning to alcohol to block out or erase his pain. Attempting to manage one's losses and grief in this way is, at best, only a temporary mode of coping. It does not alter the situation; when one sobers up, the pain remains unaltered.

Forewarning and Anticipation

To be forewarned about the likelihood of a possible loss is to be alerted to the fact that it might occur at some point in the future. Sudden, unexpected deaths by definition rule out the possibility of forewarning. In the cases considered here, however, the Wagners and the Sullivans had been warned by their physicians of the likelihood of Joan's and Julie's deaths. At first, they were reluctant to accept those warnings. All of us throughout our lives hear warnings about things that might happen. Often we dismiss such warnings or do not take them too seriously. Sometimes we acknowledge a warning but assume that the potential loss is not as bad as it might seem or that it will not occur until some time in the distant future. In their initial reactions, the Wagners and Sullivans illustrate that forewarning does not mean that the death will be anticipated or accepted, at least not at first and for some people never.

This fact is important for family members and professional and volunteer care providers to understand. It helps explain why persons who are warned of the likelihood of their own death or the death of someone they love may not acknowledge the warning or act on it. For example, they may not complete advance directives, engage in end-of-life planning, or take steps to ensure that people or projects they value will be taken care of after a death. In other words, forewarning is not a sufficient condition for realistic anticipation. Anticipation depends on forewarning, but forewarning does not necessarily lead to anticipation. If one had no forewarning or reason to expect that a death or other loss might occur, one would have no reason to anticipate its occurrence. One might have a pessimistic outlook about the future or even be anxious about what might lie ahead, but that would not necessarily lead to anticipatory grief and mourning.

Forewarning eventually led Poe, the Wagners, and Carol Sullivan to anticipate the death of the person they loved. That anticipation led to grief reactions and coping processes. Only Joe Sullivan was unwilling until the last moment to accept the likelihood of his daughter's death. He did not fully believe the warnings he received, choosing instead to try to manage the situation by seeking ways to discount those warnings and somehow save his daughter's life.

Grief and Mourning in Relation to Anticipated Loss

As noted previously, Rando (1988) suggested that the adjective "anticipatory" is not always used correctly when people speak or write about anticipatory grief and mourning. In the course of an illness or dying trajectory, those who are involved will experience a shifting series of losses. At any point in the process, some losses will already have occurred, others will be in process, and some will be in the future. Only the future losses can properly be said to be anticipated. Thus, although many things were happening while Joan Wagner was dying, not all of them were about loss and not all the losses could be described as anticipated.

For example, when the Wagners decided to enroll Joan in a hospice program, they did so in recognition of the heightened level of care she required. Joan needed more care because she had already experienced a number of losses—she had lost energy and become weaker, she had given up her job, and she was bedfast. These are all past losses with which Joan and Ned appeared to have come to terms. Including them in the sphere of anticipatory grief and mourning stretches the concept of "anticipation" beyond recognition.

The future was becoming clearer to Joan and Ned, but they might not have been able to fully appreciate it until they started living it. They discussed their expectations with the hospice staff who tried to help them develop realistic ideas about what lay ahead, at least in the short term. As they formed those ideas, they experienced grief reactions and mourning processes related to the losses they anticipated, including Joan's death but also other losses they expected to occur in the interim, such as increased physical discomfort, problems with memory or recognition of others, slipping into a coma, and missed opportunities to be part of treasured events.

Grief and Mourning: Before and After a Death

A great deal of confusion exists about grief and mourning before a death and after a death. Misunderstanding of the relationship between pre-death and post-death experiences results in misinterpretation of anticipatory grief and mourning. Such misinterpretation has led some research and clinical responses astray.

Fulton once characterized the misunderstood links as the "hydrological theory of grief." He meant that we act as if grief were a large bucket of tears; if we could pour out some of the tears before the death occurs, we would have fewer to pour out after it occurs. Thus, many researchers have focused attention on anticipatory grief and mourning in the hope that it will somehow remove or at least reduce the need for grief and mourning after the death. In fact, grief and mourning address different realities before and after a death. As Fulton (2003, p. 348) wrote, "'Anticipatory grief' is not simply grief begun in advance: it is different from post-mortem grief both in duration and form."

Consider again the example of Edgar Allan Poe. His anticipatory grief involved depression, what he called a type of insanity, and a "horrible never-ending oscillation between hope & despair." All this occurred while Virginia Poe was still alive. Her death provided Poe with "a permanent cure" and "a new but—oh God! how melancholy an existence." Because the losses he experienced and the challenges he faced before and after his wife's death were quite different, his pre-death and post-death grief and mourning also differed in significant ways.

Many people in our society die at an advanced age from degenerative or chronic diseases that involve a long dying trajectory. Family members usually are warned when death is the likely outcome, and many experience anticipatory grief and mourning. Still, as they often report, when these deaths actually take place, they find themselves encountering a new reality with a new form of grief and a new need to mourn. Some are surprised when this happens, but knowledgeable care providers explain that now they are grieving and mourning the finality of death and the new losses that follow. When it actually occurs, death and its aftermath evoke reactions and responses that family members might not have expected.

Anticipatory grief and mourning are responses to the expectation of death or loss; postmortem grief and mourning are after-the-fact responses to the reality of that death or loss. Once the anticipated loss has occurred, postmortem grief and mourning may last from the moment of death through the rest of the bereaved person's life.

Not Just Death

Anticipatory grief and mourning are most often associated with death-related losses. However, an illness or dying trajectory will most often include many losses and challenges. Any of those losses can evoke anticipatory grief reactions and anticipatory mourning tasks or processes. Death itself need not be the sole focus of anticipatory grief and mourning.

Furthermore, anticipatory grief and mourning are not exclusively restricted to death-related events. Many experiences in life can evoke grief reactions and mourning responses. A person might be facing the amputation of a body part, the termination of a cherished social status, the end of a relationship with a significant other, the birth of a handicapped child, the need to euthanize a cherished pet, or the threat of an approaching hurricane. What is common in all of these and many other experiences of significant loss is the sense that one is about to be stripped of something that is valued, that one feels bereft, and that one must begin to contemplate ways to live without that which will soon be taken away. The fact of the loss, one's perception of its value, the multiple dimensions that it often entails, and the disruption or disequilibrium that it imposes on one's life are all central to grief reactions and mourning responses. Whenever one expects a loss of this type, one may experience anticipatory grief and mourning.

Guidelines for Care Providers

Here are guidelines for anyone who is providing care to persons who are experiencing anticipatory grief and mourning.

- Be available; be present; listen. People who are experiencing anticipatory grief and mourning may or may not share with you their reactions and responses to the losses they are experiencing and anticipating, but they will never do so if you are not available and actively listening. Ask questions and make open-ended observations that encourage them to share their concerns. Listen to what they say . . . and to what they do not say. Pay attention to verbal and nonverbal communications, to literal and symbolic disclosures.
- Meet people where they are. Acknowledge that it is appropriate for them to grieve and mourn when anticipating major losses, because these losses are important and may even be life-changing for them and their families.
- Prepare yourself to encounter grief reactions in various forms: physical, psychological (cognitive and affective), behavioral, social, and spiritual. Do not limit or fail to appreciate a person's grief reactions because of preconceptions or misunderstandings about anticipatory grief.
- Allow persons who are experiencing and expressing any of the broad range of anticipatory grief reactions described earlier in this chapter to do so in whatever ways they need; only reactions that are directly harmful to the person or to others are inappropriate.
- Allow persons who are engaged in anticipatory mourning responses (e.g., tasks and/or processes as described earlier) to their expected losses to do so in whatever ways they need. Do not limit or fail to appreciate all of a person's mourning tasks and processes because of preconceptions or misunderstandings about anticipatory mourning, or lack of appreciation for individual, familial, social, ethnic, or religious customs. Allow those who are involved in anticipatory mourning tasks and processes to do so in whatever ways they need; only tasks and processes that are directly harmful to the person or to others are inappropriate.

- Expect to encounter different perspectives. Some people may be experiencing anticipatory grief and mourning, while others may not. Different people may view anticipated losses in quite different ways.
- Expect the passage of time and changes in the situation to affect anticipatory grief and mourning. Ask what the primary focus of concern is for each individual at the present moment. Do not be surprised if the focus of concern changes at different times and in different situations. Life is not static; neither are anticipatory grief and mourning. Assess and reassess each time you come to offer help.
- Even during an illness or dying trajectory, loss, grief, and mourning are not likely to take up the whole of a person's life. Anticipatory grief and mourning are only part of the larger processes of coping with dying, which are themselves only part of overall experiences in living (Corr & Corr, 2000). Anniversaries and holidays may be celebrated, reconciliations may be achieved, "unfinished business" and last wishes may be pursued. Dying persons and those who are anticipating other losses are human beings with their own priorities. Pressures associated with impending death may make the available time especially precious.
- Providing care and being cared for by persons who are experiencing anticipatory grief and mourning are important roles for family members and close friends, although they may benefit from support from trained volunteers and professionals.
- Much can be done to minimize distress and improve quality of life for persons who are experiencing anticipatory grief and mourning. Help is best offered on the basis of a realistic assessment of one's own strengths and limitations, and with the support of an interdisciplinary team of helpers who can draw on each other's strengths and limitations. Enabling people to grieve as they should and cope as they must is the noble work of helping in a context of life-threatening illness and anticipated losses.
- The more we can learn about anticipatory grief and mourning, the better we will be as helpers and as fellow human beings. In the long term, better understanding and appreciation are a constant goal; in the short term, heightened sensitivity and genuine caring are most highly prized. As Carl Jung once said about theories in psychology, "[W]e need certain points of view for their orienting and heuristic value; but they should always be regarded as mere auxiliary concepts that can be laid aside at any time" (1954, p. 7).

Concluding Thoughts

Grief reactions to anticipated death or loss are neither inherently positive nor negative. Everything depends on the nature of the reaction, how it is experienced, and how it is expressed. Similarly, engaging in anticipatory mourning to cope with impending death or loss is neither inherently positive nor negative. Everything depends on whether the coping tasks and processes promote productive living before and after the death or loss is realized.

For the most part, anticipatory grief and mourning are healthy and constructive experiences. As a general rule, it is better to have some time, awareness of what is happening and is likely to happen, legitimization of anticipatory grief reactions, and opportunities to engage in constructive forms of anticipatory mourning than to be confronted by a sudden, unanticipated death or loss. Anticipation can provide opportunities to prepare for expected events, to develop productive coping strategies, and to mobilize assistance. We should not minimize opportunities for people to experience anticipatory grief and mourning. Nor should we minimize the roles of those who are privileged to foster understanding, offer support, and provide help to these persons.

Editor's Note: This chapter was revised from Corr, C. A. (2007). Anticipatory grief and mourning: An overview. In K. J. Doka (Ed.), *Living with grief: Before and after the death*, Washington, DC: Hospice Foundation of America.

***

Charles A. Corr, *PhD, is vice-chair of the Board of Directors of the Suncoast Institute (an affiliate of Suncoast Hospice). He is a member of the ChiPPS (Children's Project on Palliative/Hospice Services) Communications Work Group of the National Hospice and Palliative Care Organization; the Executive Committee of the National Donor Family Council; the Association for Death Education and Counseling; and the International Work Group on Death, Dying, and Bereavement (Chairperson, 1989-93). He is also professor emeritus, Southern Illinois University Edwardsville. Dr. Corr's publications in the field of death, dying, and bereavement include three dozen books and booklets, along with more than 110 chapters and articles in professional publications. His next book, the seventh edition of* Death and Dying, Life and Living *(Belmont, CA: Wadsworth), co-authored with Donna M. Corr, will be published in January 2012.*

REFERENCES

Aldrich, C. K. (1963). The dying patient's grief. *Journal of the American Medical Association, 184,* 329–331.

Corr, C. A., & Corr, D. M. (2000). Anticipatory mourning and coping with dying: Similarities, differences, and suggested guidelines for helpers. In T. A. Rando (Ed.). (2000a), *Clinical dimensions of anticipatory mourning: Theory and practice in working with the dying, their loved ones, and their caregivers* (pp. 223–251). Champaign, IL: Research Press.

Doka, K. J. (Ed.). (1989). *Disenfranchised grief: Recognizing hidden sorrow.* Lexington, MA: Lexington Books.

Doka, K. J. (Ed.). (2002). *Disenfranchised grief: New directions, strategies, and challenges for practice.* Champaign, IL: Research Press.

Elias, N. (1991). On human beings and their emotions: A process-sociological essay. In M. Featherstone, M. Hepworth, & B. S. Turner (Eds.), *The body: Social process and cultural theory* (pp. 103–125). London: Sage.

Fulton, R. (2003). Anticipatory mourning: A critique of the concept. *Mortality, 8,* 342–351.

Fulton, R., & Fulton, J. (1971). A psychosocial aspect of terminal care: Anticipatory grief. *Omega: Journal of Death and Dying, 2,* 91–100.

Fulton, R., & Fulton, J. (1972). Anticipatory grief: A psychosocial aspect of terminal care. In B. Schoenberg, A. C. Carr, D. Peretz, & A. H. Kutscher (Eds.), *Psychosocial aspects of terminal care* (pp. 227–242). New York: Columbia University Press.

Fulton, R., & Gottesman, D. J. (1980). Anticipatory grief: A psychosocial concept reconsidered. *British Journal of Psychiatry, 137,* 45–54.

Futterman, E. H., Hoffman, I., & Sabshin, M. (1972). Parental anticipatory mourning. In B. Schoenberg, A. C. Carr, D. Peretz, & A. H. Kutscher (Eds.), *Psychosocial aspects of terminal care* (pp. 243–272). New York: Columbia University Press.

Jung, C. G. (1954). The development of personality (Vol. 17). In H. Read, M. Fordham, & G. Adler (Eds.), *The collected works of C. G. Jung* (2nd ed.; 20 vols.). New York: Pantheon.

Lindemann, E. (1944). Symptomatology and management of acute grief. *American Journal of Psychiatry, 101,* 143–148.

Poe, E. A. (1948). *The letters of Edgar Allan Poe* (2 vols.). J. W. Ostrom (Ed.). Cambridge, MA: Harvard University Press.

Rando, T. A. (Ed.). (1986). *Loss and anticipatory grief.* Lexington, MA: Lexington Books.

Rando, T. A. (1988). Anticipatory grief: The term is a misnomer but the phenomenon exists. *Journal of Palliative Care, 4*(1/2), 70–73.

Rando, T. A. (Ed.). (2000a). *Clinical dimensions of anticipatory mourning: Theory and practice in working with the dying, their loved ones, and their caregivers.* Champaign, IL: Research Press.

Rando, T. A. (2000b). Anticipatory mourning: A review and critique of the literature. In T. A. Rando (Ed.), *Clinical dimensions of anticipatory mourning: Theory and practice in working with the dying, their loved ones, and their caregivers* (pp. 17–50). Champaign, IL: Research Press.

Schoenberg, B., Carr, A., Kutscher, A. H., Peretz, D., & Goldberg, I. (Eds.). (1974). *Anticipatory grief.* New York: Columbia University Press.

Siegel, K., & Weinstein, L. (1983). Anticipatory grief reconsidered. *Journal of Psychosocial Oncology, 1,* 61–73.

Sourkes, B. M. (1996). The broken heart: Anticipatory grief in the child facing death. *Journal of Palliative Care, 12*(3), 56–59.

CHAPTER 3

Task Models and the Dying Process

Kenneth J. Doka

The 1969 publication of Kübler-Ross's *On Death and Dying* was a seminal event in the development of the field of thanatology. While not the first work in the field, the book fully caught the public imagination. In that work, Kübler-Ross posited that dying persons went through a series of five stages—*denial, anger, bargaining, depression,* and *acceptance*. Kübler-Ross stressed that within and all through these stages *hope* was a constant reaction—though the content of hope may change from "perhaps I will beat this" to "I hope I see my brother before I die." These stages were subsequently applied to a wide range of situations including grief (Kübler-Ross & Kessler, 2005). The Stage Theory became so widely known and accepted that it became the predominant model taught in nursing schools (Coolican, Stark, Doka, & Corr, 1994). The model was so well known and accepted by the general public that it appeared in popular culture, serving as a basis of episodes for such television shows as *Frasier* and *The Simpsons* and providing the structure of Bob Fosse's film *All That Jazz*.

Kübler-Ross's *On Death and Dying* appeared at the right moment with the right message. Kübler-Ross was a charismatic woman who spoke of a "natural death" at a time when there was an increased aversion to technological and impersonal care (Klass & Hutton, 1985). In that cultural context, her message found a ready audience.

Moreover, the concept of stages has a long history in the human sciences—exemplified by the work of developmental theorists such as Freud (1917), Kohlberg (1984), and Erickson (1963). The appeal of a stage theory is understandable. Stages offer a level of predictability to an otherwise chaotic event. In Kübler-Ross's case, the theory offered a sense that a frightening event—dying—could be managed; that is, that patients could be brought from denial to acceptance (Klass & Hutton, 1985). As Neimeyer indicates in his chapter, the very stage theory of dying may even have a deeper resonance. It mimics the structure of a classic epic where the hero has to undergo a series of difficult trials on a journey that promises deeper understanding.

Kübler-Ross's Stage Theory, though still popular in lay literature, is now recognized as problematic and inadequate as a way to understand the ways that individuals cope with the dying process. Evaluations of her theory of stages (e.g., Doka, 2009) note many problems. Some are methodological in nature. Kübler-Ross never fully documented her material or her methodology; it is unclear how her data were collected or how many patients experienced which reactions. Nor has research supported the concept of stages (e.g., Schulz & Aderman, 1974).

There are other problems as well. While Kübler-Ross insisted that the Stage Theory was not to be understood literally or linearly, the book clearly offers an impression of linear stages. In addition, it is unclear whether the stages represent a description of how persons cope with dying or a prescriptive approach that stresses that dying individuals ought to be assisted to move through the five stages and eventually embrace acceptance. By positing universal stages, individual differences and the diverse ways that persons cope with dying were ignored.

Perhaps the most significant criticism of the stage theory of dying is that denial and acceptance were far more complex than presented by Kübler-Ross (Weisman, 1972). In Kübler-Ross's work, denial was essentially a negative state—a buffer brought on through shock of a terminal diagnosis. The dying patient had first to surmount this denial, to recognize, even in an existential anger, that death was imminent, and thereby to begin the journey toward a more peaceful acceptance or, at the very least, a passive resignation to death.

However, other studies indicated that denial was much more complex. Weisman (1972) described *orders of denial*, emphasizing that patients might deny a number of realities in the course of the illness. In *first-order denial*, the patient denies the symptom. For example, the patient may deny a lump or a lesion, insisting that it was always there or the result of an injury that will soon heal. A patient in *second-order denial* no longer denies the symptom, but denies some aspect of the diagnosis. *Third-order denial* means that the patient accepts the diagnosis while avoiding the prognosis that usually accompanies it. While delineating the complexity of denial, Weisman also notes that denial is not always negative. It allows patients to participate in therapy and sustain hope. Denial is a defense mechanism. In the absence of denial at some level, there is little reason to engage in painful therapies.

Weisman introduced a very significant concept of *middle knowledge*—meaning that patients drift in and out of denial; sometimes affirming, other times denying the closeness of death. Denial then is not a state that patients leave on a journey to acceptance. Rather it is a constant companion as patients deal with the reality of illness. Persons even in the later of stages of illness may deny the possibility of death in one conversation even as they acknowledge it in the next. The concept of *middle knowledge* considerably expands the understanding of denial. It reminds us that individuals with life-threatening illness must, at times, use denial simply to cope with the realities of life—one could not constantly focus on one's own death. Yet, as Weisman also points out, true and sustained denial in persons with life-threatening illness is rare. Such individuals, even children, are constantly assessing internal cues. They know they are getting weaker, they can feel the disease progress. They are reminded of their condition by external cues, the visits, glances, and guarded comments of others. In an Internet era, information is no longer controlled by medical monopoly; it is easily available by a few clicks of a mouse.

To Weisman the important question was not "Does the patient accept or deny death?" but rather "When, with whom, and under what circumstances does the patient discuss the possibility of death?"

Yet despite these serious criticisms, Kübler-Ross, in her many case vignettes, offered a model of communication that made a powerful plea for the humanistic care of the dying patient. In an excellent evaluation of Kübler-Ross' contributions, Corr, in his chapter, suggests that this call for humanistic care and her affirming message to talk to dying persons, along with the heuristic value of the work, remain the enduring legacies of *On Death and Dying*.

DYING AS A PROCESS

One of the limitations of Kübler-Ross's work is that in the time it was written, many individuals diagnosed with a disease had a limited life span and dealt with her or his disease exclusively within a medical setting. As time and treatment progressed, the reality of illness changed. A diagnosis in many diseases was not necessarily a death sentence. Individuals experienced treatment, often as an outpatient, and even returned to their earlier roles. Theories have to consider the entire process inherent in a struggle with a life-limiting or life-threatening illness.

Both Pattison's (1978) and Weisman's (1980) work began to reflect the changing nature of the illness experience. Pattison (1978) spoke of a *living-dying interval*, or the time between a diagnosis and a death. As Pattison noted over 30 years ago, this is a new stage in the human lifecycle, enabled by medical advances that allowed individuals to extend life considerably. In the years since Pattison first wrote about the living-dying interval, not only has this time been extended but, for many diseases, even the certainty of death has been challenged.

Pattison further divided this living-dying interval into three phases. The first phase, an *Acute Crisis Phase,* is characterized by the crisis of a diagnosis that disrupts the assumptions and patterns of life. The *Chronic Phase* is the period of time where one lives with the disease, seeks treatment, and copes with a multiplicity of fears as the disease continues to progress. In the *Terminal Phase,* the patient begins to disengage as he or she approaches death.

Similarly Weisman (1980), studying cancer patients, spoke of a number of stages in the course of the illness. The first of Weisman's Psychosocial Stages of Cancer was *Existential Plight.* Here there are two sub-stages—*impact distress* at the time of diagnosis and *existential plight proper* as the patient continues to adjust to the diagnosis, initial treatment, the reality of cancer, and the threat of death. Weisman recognizes that some of these fears and issues can even arise prior to diagnosis as the patient begins to notice signs and possibly suspect cancer. This phase usually lasts about three or four months.

The second stage, *Mitigation and Accommodation,* can last indefinitely depending on the course of the disease. Here essentially the patient learns to live with the diagnosis, adjusting to the limitations imposed by the treatment or the cancer itself.

Stage three, *Decline and Deterioration,* occurs when the disease progresses. Here the patient's quality of life begins to suffer and the patient moves to a fourth stage, *Terminality and Preterminality,* as the declines become steeper and death becomes inevitable. It is critical to reiterate that Weisman did not see these stages as driven by the emotional needs of the patient but rather the progression of the disease.

Myers and Lynn (2001) remind us of another reality of death in contemporary Western societies. Many people today, especially older persons, face multiple, chronic, life-threatening illnesses as they approach the end of life. This reality not only complicates care; it makes a definitive prognosis difficult. The result is that many individuals today die *suddenly*—in the midst of multiple chronic conditions. Stage models then have even less relevance to this new reality of dying.

The Development of Task Models

As research in thanatology continued, the inadequacies of the stage model became evident. Scholars began to acknowledge that rather than attempt to find universal stages, theories had to account for the personal pathways individuals experienced as they encountered illness, loss, and grief. Worden (1982, 2009) offered a "Task Model" of grief. Worden began with the assumption that rather than a common set of reactions, bereaved individuals faced common problems or issues.

> Task I: To Accept the Reality of the Loss
> Task II: To Process the Pain of Grief
> Task III: To Adjust to a World Without the Deceased
> Task IV: To Find an Enduring Connection With the Deceased in the Midst of Embarking on a New Life

Worden's Task Model found ready acceptance, and his book, *Grief Counseling and Grief Therapy: A Handbook for the Mental Health Practitioner* became a basic and enduring text in the field. There were a number of reasons for this. First, Worden in each edition was willing to modify his approach to incorporate the latest research. For example, in the first edition, Worden (1982) described the fourth task as to "withdraw emotional energy from the deceased and reinvest it in others" (p. 50)—a representation of Freud's (1917) notion of grief work. Yet as subsequent research (e.g., Klass, Silverman, & Nickman, 1996; Silverman, Nickman, & Worden, 1992) indicated deficiencies in this approach—stressing instead that individuals retained a continuing bond with the deceased—Worden (2009) revised his fourth task so it now reads: "To find an enduring connection with the deceased in the midst of embarking on a new life" (p. 50).

There were other strengths to a Task Model. It acknowledged the individuality of the grief process. While individuals may have to address common issues as they encounter loss, they do so in an idiosyncratic way. Each person may have his or her own reactions and adaptations as they undertake the tasks. As with any set of tasks, some may be easier to tackle while others are more problematic. Some persons may struggle as they process the emotions inherent in loss while others may have difficulty in coping with life without the deceased.

In addition, the Task Model does not assume linearity. Though labeled Task I, Task II, etc., there is no inherent order to these tasks. This again affirms the individuality of the model. Individuals will choose the task work they are competent and comfortable to do. Moreover, the model has significant therapeutic value, by offering counselors a paradigm to assess the issues that an individual is struggling with in grief, allowing focused interventions to address a given task. In a similar way, it offers models for psycho-education and group support in grief—reminding counselors that it is insufficient to focus only on emotional work as that is only one of the issues inherent in loss.

TASK MODELS OF THE DYING PROCESS

Since the Task Model proved to be an effective way to conceptualize the grieving process, it was eventually applied to assist in understanding the issues of individuals struggling with dying or life-threatening illness. Both Corr (1992) and Doka (1995, 2009) applied the concept of tasks to the dying process. To Corr (1992), individuals coping with dying had to respond to four major tasks that corresponded to the dimensions of human life—physical, psychological, social, and spiritual. The physical task was "to satisfy bodily needs and to minimize physical distress in ways that are consistent with other values" (p. 85). Corr emphasizes that unless symptom control and pain relief are adequately accomplished, the patient is unlikely to focus on other needs. Yet Corr also affirms that other issues and values may, at times, be primary to the patient.

This leads to the psychological issue of maintaining a sense of autonomy and control even at a physically challenging time. Corr defined the psychological task as "to maximize psychological security, autonomy, and richness" (p. 85). This control is one critical psychological issue. Others include a need to feel safe and secure that one will not be abandoned, as well as a need for psychological richness, individually defined, even as life ebbs.

The social task was "to sustain and enhance those interpersonal attachments that are significant to the person concerned, and to address the social implications of dying (i.e., sustain selected interactions with social groups within society or with society itself)" (p. 85). These include maintaining meaningful personal ties as well as retaining a connection to the larger society, and possibly utilizing effectively the resources of collective organizations such as governmental entities or spiritual bodies.

Corr's spiritual task was "to address issues of meaningfulness, connectedness, and transcendence and, in doing so, to foster hope" (p. 85). This ultimately entails, to Corr, reaching a sense of what Erikson (1963) called *ego integrity*—a sense that one's life had meaning and purpose. Corr also defines *hope* as an essential aspect of spiritual care—acknowledging that the focus of hope may change in the course of an illness from perhaps a miraculous cure to a hope for a final reconciliation with an estranged family member or friend or a hope for reunion in an afterlife.

Building on the work of both Pattison (1978) and Weisman (1980), Doka (1995, 2009) too proposed a task model but suggested that a life-threatening illness could be understood as a series of phases, noting that not all phases would appear in any given illness (1995). The *Pre-diagnostic Phase* concerns itself with the process of health seeking, and refers to the time prior to the diagnosis. One of the most common times, but not the only one, would be the time between when an individual notices a symptom and seeks medical assistance. The *Acute Phase* refers to the crisis period surrounding the diagnosis of life-threatening illness. The *Chronic Phase* refers to that period where the individual struggles with the disease and treatment. Many individuals may recover from the illness. However, it is important to remember that in the *Recovery Phase*, individuals do not simply go back to the life experienced before illness. They still have to adapt to the aftereffects, residues, and fears and anxieties aroused by the illness. The *Terminal Phase* revolves around adapting to the inevitability of impending death as treatment becomes palliative.

At each phase, individuals have to adapt to a series of tasks. These tasks derive from four general or global tasks—*to respond to the physical facts of disease; to take steps to cope with the reality of the disease; to preserve self-concept and relationships with others in the face of the disease; and to deal with affective and existential/spiritual issues created or reactivated by the disease.*

A *Pre-diagnostic Phase* often precedes diagnosis. Here, someone recognizes symptoms or risk factors that make him or her prone to the illness. That person now needs to select strategies to cope with this threat. The tasks here include:
1. Recognizing possible danger or risk
2. Coping with anxiety and uncertainty
3. Developing and following through on a health-seeking strategy.

The *Acute Phase* centers on the crisis of diagnosis. At this point an individual is faced with a diagnosis of life-threatening illness and must make a series of decisions—medical, psychological, interpersonal, and so on—about how, at least initially, to cope with the crisis. Here the tasks include:
1. Understanding the disease
2. Examining and maximizing health and lifestyle
3. Maximizing one's coping strengths and limiting weaknesses

4. Examining internal and external resources and liabilities
5. Developing strategies to deal with issues created by disease (disclosure, coping with professionals, treatment options, life contingencies)
6. Exploring the effect of illness on one's sense of self and relationships with others
7. Ventilating feelings and fears
8. Integrating the present reality of the diagnosis with one's past life and future plans.

In the *Chronic Phase*, the individual is struggling with the disease and its treatment. Many people in this phase may be attempting, with varying degrees of success, to live a reasonably normal life within the confines of the disease. Often this period is punctuated by a series of illness-related crisis. Tasks in this phase include:
1. Managing symptoms and side effects
2. Carrying out health regimens
3. Preventing and managing health crises
4. Managing stress and examining coping
5. Maximizing social support and minimizing social isolation
6. Normalizing life in the face of disease
7. Dealing with financial concerns
8. Preserving self-concept
9. Redefining relationships with others
10. Ventilating feeling and fears
11. Finding meaning in suffering, chronicity, uncertainty, and decline.

In many cases people will not experience all of these phases. Sometimes in the acute or chronic phase, or even rarely in the terminal phase, a person may experience recovery. This is a *Recovery/Remission Phase*. Even here, however, people may have to cope with certain tasks such as:
1. Dealing with psychological, social, spiritual, and financial after-effects of illness
2. Coping with fears and anxieties about recurrence
3. Examining life and life-style issues and reconstructing one's life
4. Redefining relationships with caregivers.

The *Terminal Phase* describes the situation in which the disease has progressed to a point where death is inevitable. Death is no longer merely possible; now

it is likely. Death has become the individual's and family's central crisis. Tasks here include:
1. Dealing with symptoms, discomfort, pain, and incapacitation
2. Managing health procedures and institutional procedures
3. Managing stress and examining coping
4. Dealing effectively with caregivers
5. Preparing for death and saying good-bye
6. Preserving self-concept
7. Preserving appropriate relationships with family and friends
8. Ventilating feelings and fears
9. Finding meaning in life and death.

Conclusion

As Corr (1992) notes, Task Models offer certain inherent advantages over Stage-Based Models. First, Task Models are holistic insofar as the tasks include not only emotions but all aspects of coping with a given experience. Second, such models also allow generalization while preserving individuality. Third, task-based approaches are empowering. Individuals are not seen as swept inexorably into a set of preordained stages but rather are constantly making decisions on how they will deal with issues that arise within the process. Finally, such an approach gives guidance to counselors reiterating that a valid role is to assist patients and their caregivers as they adapt to the challenges or tasks posited by the illness experience.

Though these models seem to have interesting implications for understanding the ways that individuals cope with dying and life-threatening illness, they have not been widely applied, perhaps because they do not offer the simplicity of Stage Models. It is critical to remember that they speak to limited aspects of the dying process—the process of dying and the ways that individuals, their intimate networks, and their professional caregivers cope with dying. A comprehensive theoretical model of dying would address other issues including communication, ethical decision-making, continuation and transformation of identity within the dying process, palliative care, and the ways that families and even care facilities such as hospitals and hospices maintain continuity in the face of death (Corr, Doka, & Kastenbaum, 1999). Yet, while stage models of the dying process, though historically significant, now seem limited in what they can offer, task models still represent a possible basis for the development of new approaches and paradigms of the dying process. The ultimate test of any model remains whether it recognizes what ultimately is a highly individual process, and still makes coping with dying and illness more understandable to those experiencing it and those who seek to help.

Editor's Note: This chapter deals from material originally published in Doka, K.J. (2009). *Counseling individuals with life-threatening illness*. New York: Springer Publishing Co.

Kenneth J. Doka, PhD, MDiv, *is a professor of gerontology at the Graduate School of The College of New Rochelle and senior consultant to the Hospice Foundation of America. A prolific author and editor, Dr. Doka serves as editor of HFA's* Living with Grief® *book series, its* Journeys *newsletter, and numerous other books and publications. Dr. Doka has served as a panelist on HFA's* Living with Grief® *video programs for 17 years. Dr. Doka was elected president of the Association for Death Education and Counseling (ADEC) in 1993. In 1995, he was elected to the Board of Directors of the International Work Group on Death, Dying, and Bereavement and served as its chair from 1997–99. ADEC presented him with an award for Outstanding Contributions in the Field of Death Education in 1998. In 2006, Dr. Doka was grandfathered in as a mental health counselor under New York's first state licensure of counselors. Dr. Doka is an ordained Lutheran minister.*

REFERENCES

Coolican, M. B., Stark, J., Doka, K. J., & Corr, C. A. (1994). Education about death, dying, and bereavement in nursing programs. *Nurse Education, 19*(6), 35–40.

Corr, C. A. (1992). A task-based approach to coping with dying. *Omega: Journal of Death and Dying, 25,* 81–94.

Corr, C. A., Doka, K. J, & Kastenbaum, R. (1999). Dying and its interpreters: A review of selected literature and some comments on the state of the field. *Omega: Journal of Death and Dying, 39,* 239–259.

Doka, K. J. (1995). Coping with life-threatening illness: A Task Based Approach. *Omega: Journal of Death and Dying, 32,* 111–122.

Doka, K. J. (2009). *Counseling individuals with life-threatening illness*. New York: Springer Publishing Co.

Erikson, E. H. (1963). *Childhood and society* (2nd ed.). New York: Norton.

Freud, S. (1957). Mourning and melancholia. In J. Strachey (Ed. and Trans.), *The standard edition of the complete psychological works of Sigmund Freud* (Vol. 14, pp. 237–260). London, England: Hogarth Press. (Original work published 1917).

Freud, S. (1986). Some thoughts on development and regression—Aetiology. In J. Strachey (Ed. and Trans.), *The standard edition of the complete psychological works of Sigmund Freud* (Vol. 16, pp. 339–357). London, England: Hogarth Press. (Original work published 1917).

Klass, D., & Hutton, R. A. (1985). Elisabeth Kübler-Ross as a religious leader. *Omega: Journal of Death and Dying, 16,* 89–109.

Klass, D., Silverman, P. R., & Nickman, S. (Eds.). (1996). *Continuing bonds: New understandings of grief.* Taylor & Francis: Washington DC & London.

Kohlberg, L. (1984). *The psychology of moral development.* San Francisco: Harper & Row.

Kübler-Ross, E. (1969). *On death and dying.* New York: Macmillan.

Kübler-Ross, E., & Kessler, D. (2005). *On grief and grieving: Finding the meaning of grief through the five stages of loss.* New York: Scribners.

Myers, S. S., & Lynn, J. (2001). Patients with eventually fatal chronic illness: Their importance within a national research agenda on improving patient safety and reducing medical error. *Journal of Palliative Medicine, 4,* 325–332.

Pattison, E. M. (1978). The living-dying interval. In C. Garfield, (Ed.), *Psychological care of the dying patient* (pp. 163–168). New York: McGraw-Hill.

Schulz, R., & Aderman, D. (1974). Clinical research and the stages of dying. *Omega: Journal of Death and Dying, 5,* 137–143.

Silverman, P., Nickman, S., & Worden, J. W. (1992). Detachment revisited: The child's reconstruction of a dead parent. *American Journal of Orthopsychiatry, 62,* 494–503.

Weisman, A. (1972). *On dying and denying. A psychiatric study of terminality.* New York: Behavioral Publications.

Weisman, A. (1980). Thanatology. In O. Kaplan (Ed.), *Comprehensive textbook of psychiatry.* Baltimore: Williams and Williams.

Worden, J. W. (1982). *Grief counseling and grief therapy: A handbook for the mental health practitioner.* New York: Springer.

Worden, J. W. (2009). *Grief counseling and grief therapy: A handbook for the mental health practitioner* (4th Ed.). New York: Springer.

PART II

New Perspectives on Grief

In many ways, our understanding of grief has changed dramatically in the last 40 years. Not only has there been a move away from models emphasizing universal stages of grief, but there has also been a reconsideration of Freud's classic work on "Mourning and Melancholia" (1917). The concept of the "grief work hypothesis," derived from Freud—the notion that one has to work through painful feelings in order to detach emotional energy from the deceased and reinvest that energy in others—is now severely challenged.

Kenneth Doka begins this section with a chapter that offers an overview of these significant changes. To Doka, our understanding of grief has changed in a number of ways—extending the understanding of grief from reaction to a death of a family member to a more inclusive understanding of loss; from viewing grief reactions as universal stages to a recognition of personal pathways; from seeing grief as affect to recognizing the multiple and multifaceted reactions that persons have toward loss and the ways that responses to grief are influenced by culture, gender, and spirituality; from coping passively with loss to seeing the possibilities of transformation and growth in mourning; moving from an understanding that grief involves relinquishing ties to incorporating an idea of continuing bonds; and finally from understanding grief as simply a normal transitional issue to recognizing more complicated variants and the necessity for careful assessment.

These ideas are further developed in David Balk's chapter. Balk reviews a number of new models and trends in our understanding of grief. A great value in Balk's chapter is showing the long historical development that underlies our changing understanding of grief. In fact Balk's chapter offers a *tour de force* through that history—indicating a consistent theoretical development of the ideas of Freud in the work of Lindemann, Bowlby, and Worden, noting, of course, the continued evolution of Worden's Task Model of Grief. Balk implies that Kübler-Ross's Stage Theory was a departure from this long intellectual development, albeit one that captured the public imagination. Balk includes a discussion of contemporary conceptual developments such as the Dual Process Model as well as recent research that continues to challenge the grief work hypothesis.

Richard Tedeschi, Lawrence Calhoun, and Elizabeth Addington explore the opportunities for change—even growth—that can occur in loss. Tedeschi, Calhoun, and Addington do not minimize the pain inherent in loss even as they recognize that such adversity can be a source of *posttraumatic growth*—a term they coined. This growth can be evident in a number of dimensions including personal, relational, and spiritual. The authors recognize that such growth is not inevitable but can be assisted by expert companions, beginning with the ways that counselors approach the grieving individuals. For example, a Surviving Spouse Group posits a more active notion than a Widow and Widowers Group. Their model offers a way to reframe counseling as doing more than simply assisting persons as they cope with loss.

Paul Rosenblatt's chapter closes this section. Rosenblatt makes a valid point that as we explore grief from a cross-cultural perspective, the concept of universal stages seems, at best, naive. Rosenblatt emphasizes that loss and grief are shaped and socially constructed within a culture. Even attachments may be differently understood between cultures. Based on that analysis, Rosenblatt offers suggestions for culturally-sensitive practice. Rosenblatt ends on a familiar note—reminding readers, as did Corr—that the real contribution of Kübler-Ross, and the heart of cultural sensitivity, is to carefully listen to the stories of dying and bereaved individuals.

CHAPTER 4

Does Coping With Bereavement Occur in Stages?

David E. Balk

The grief work hypothesis has been the reigning paradigm in thanatology for nearly 100 years. Since the early 1990s empirical findings and conceptual essays have marked a continual assault on the coherence of the grief work hypothesis and on the mechanisms whereby the grief work hypothesis maintains bereavement resolution takes place. There is growing unrest to fill the theoretical and practical vacuum created by the substantive skepticism now governing belief about the grief work hypothesis. One way to tack into an investigation of these developments is to look at the central matter at stake in efforts to explain bereavement and grieving, namely, how do various models discuss the ways that individuals adapt to irreparable loss.

Recovery from bereavement, sometimes called bereavement resolution, is at the heart of the many influential models of human grieving, including the oft-maligned five stages of grieving postulated by Kübler-Ross (1969; Kübler-Ross & Kessler, 2005). Recently the focus on recovery has grown sharper as debate has swirled around whether recovery from bereavement is possible (Balk, 2008).

The various models of human bereavement and grieving that have captured our imaginations over the past century give different accounts of what recovery entails and, in some cases, how recovery occurs. I have organized the chapter into an overview of the mainstream views proposed by Freud and Bowlby, the influential models developed as commentary on Freud and Bowlby, and the recent conceptual and empirical challenges to these mainstream views.

MAINSTREAM VIEWS

The mainstream views emerge as commentary on Freud's understanding of human grieving and on what Lindemann transformed into the legacy of grief work. These mainstream views start with Freud's seminal paper on bereavement and depression, move to Lindemann's use of and transformation of Freud's ideas, include Bowlby's arguments about bereavement as part of our evolution and as a process of four phases, find expression in tasks of mourning devised by Worden as well as by Parkes and Weiss, and are identified by Kübler-Ross as occurring in five stages.

Freud on Recovery From Bereavement

Freud's ideas about bereavement and grief are well-known to persons in thanatology. He noted that the distress of bereavement mimics depression, but differs in a central way: Depression is a pathological condition whereas bereavement is a normal response to the irreparable loss of someone loved. For Freud, bereavement is a human misfortune, not a clinical situation calling for professional help. Recovery occurs slowly over time as the person grieves the loss. Grieving the loss involves three ongoing tasks: (a) the person consciously confronts all the reminders of the deceased so that gradually the distress of the loss abates; (b) the person emotionally detaches from the person who died; and (c) the person forms a mental image—a store of memories—of the deceased that does not evoke grief. Freud noted that recovering from bereavement was arduous and gradual. In short, for Freud, grief involves the reactions to being bereaved, and grieving is how one recovers from bereavement (Freud, 1917).

Lindemann's Use of and Transformation of Freud

Faced with the formidable task of assisting persons grieving the sudden deaths of 492 persons in the Cocoanut Grove fire that occurred in Boston in 1942, Erich Lindemann, a psychiatrist at Harvard University and Massachusetts General Hospital, turned to Freud's psychoanalytic model of grieving and made one major change: He identified bereavement not as a human misfortune that resolves itself over time with hard work but rather as a condition to be treated by clinical professionals.

Lindemann made a major contribution when he identified an Acute Grief Syndrome (1944) that all the persons in his treatment program manifested. Certain responses were seen to be endemic to grief, and people now had a map of the bereavement terrain: Grief involved waves of somatic distress; a sense of unreality; feelings of guilt; irritability; loss of patterns of conduct; intense preoccupations with images and thoughts of the deceased; and emotional distance from other people. These features of an acute grief syndrome gave criteria to document the extent to which a person had recovered. In Lindemann's words, how long the acute grief syndrome lasts depends on "the success with which a person does the *grief work*, namely, emancipation from the bondage to the deceased, readjustment to the environment in which the deceased is missing, and the formation of new relationships" (1944, p. 143).

Lindemann got the notion of grief work from what he read in Freud. According to Lindemann, it is absolutely essential for bereaved persons to feel the intense distress bereavement produces and to openly express the feelings that grief stimulates. Freud said resolution of bereavement required a person to encounter all reminders of the deceased person until emotional attachment had been withdrawn fully from the person. Lindemann added the requirement that persons need to give verbal expression to their grief. He noted that men particularly resisted open expression of grief and that many patients, both men and women, prefer to avoid the "intense distress connected with the grief experience" (1944, p. 143).

Lindemann said recovering from bereavement requires eight separate tasks, all tied to grief work:

1. Accept the distressing pain of bereavement
2. Review one's relationship with the person who died
3. Work through the fears of going insane triggered by surprising, intense responses (such as unexpected outbursts of hostility)
4. Understand changes in emotional responses since the death
5. Give expression to one's sorrow
6. Construct an acceptable relationship to the person who died (perhaps Lindemann is referring to Freud's mental representation of the deceased)
7. Express feelings of guilt
8. Acquire new patterns of behavior.

Bowlby's Understanding of Bereavement

John Bowlby was a British psychiatrist whose thinking about bereavement was stimulated by the effects of the Second World War. As a response to the Nazi's relentless bombing of British cities in 1939–1940, the British government decided on a drastic solution to protect children from being killed: children were removed from their parents and taken into the center of the country away from the targets of Nazi aircraft. Bowlby was asked to examine the effects this separation from parents had on children, and his whole viewpoint on bereavement stems from his work on this project.

Bowlby looked to fields other than psychology or psychiatry to find an explanatory mechanism about bereavement and its consequences. While Freud referred to psychic processes to explain our response to being irreparably separated from someone we love, Bowlby turned to ethology. Ethology involves studying animal behavior in natural environments (such as Jane Goodall's study of chimpanzees) and uses a biological perspective to study human behavior. Central in Bowlby's understanding of bereavement is his championing of Charles Darwin and the theory of evolution.

Merging ethology and an evolutionary perspective, Bowlby maintained that the survival of mammals depends on close bonds established between infants and caregivers. Caregivers and their young, vulnerable dependents become attached to each other. Such attachment bonds become prominent in higher order mammals, and mutuality characterizes the bond: It is not just that the child is attached to the parent or the parent to the child, but their relationship is defined by a mutuality of attachment bonds. These attachment bonds are biologically wired into the human species (as well as other mammalian species), and they form a survival function: the attachment bonds enable the vulnerable young to be protected, to learn, and to grow to adulthood. The types of attachment bonds a youngster has with caregivers greatly influence the kinds of attachments that the youngster will form with others over his or her life span. Bowlby explained bereavement, grief, and mourning as the responses that naturally occur when bonds of attachment are sundered (Bowlby, 1969–1980). Whereas Freud explained bereavement as the natural consequence of refusal to accept that an object of libidinal investment was lost forever, Bowlby said bereavement occurred due to the prior formation of attachment bonds. In Bowlby's thinking, without attachment bonds, there would be no bereavement.

Bowlby introduced the notion of phases to our understanding of the grieving process. He said that grieving takes four phases toward recovery:

Numbing. In this first phase, the bereaved person seems incapable of comprehending the loss. A person will say such things as, "I can't believe this has happened" or "It can't be true."

Yearning or searching. In the second phase, the bereaved person seems preoccupied with thoughts and feelings about the deceased. There is what Bowlby considered a "desire to recover the person who is now gone" (Cook & Oltjenbruns, 1989, p. 48). Sounds in the house will prompt thoughts that the person has returned. Someone who resembles the dead person may lead the bereaved individual to think they are seeing the one they miss. The phone will ring, and the person will initially think the call is from the person who has died.

Disorganization and despair. This third phase emerges as the bereaved person realizes the dead person cannot be recovered. Apathy may set in as the person struggles to find ways to cope with an irreparable loss. The challenge is to discard established patterns of thinking, feeling, and acting based on interactions prior to the person's death. The bereaved individual feels helpless and can become very vulnerable to bad advice or to unscrupulous individuals who prey on the bereaved.

Reorganization. The fourth phase of Bowlby's model denotes a time when a person begins redefining his or her identity and place in the world. Not uncommonly such reorganization requires learning new roles, as when a middle-aged widow returns to the work force after a 20-year absence or a widower learns how to cook and do laundry. According to Bowlby, reorganization denotes recovery from bereavement, and moving through the various phases is how one recovers. These four phases are how Bowlby sees grief work taking place. Criticisms of this model are its linearity and how it makes grief into a passive process one endures rather than a proactive process of engagement.

Tasks of Mourning

J. William Worden, an American clinical psychologist, has developed a very influential model that explains coping with grief in terms of four pro-active tasks to be accomplished. The first presentation of the tasks was synthesized straight from Freud and Lindemann, and called on grievers to accept the reality of the loss, work through to the pain of grief, adjust to an environment in which the deceased is missing, and withdraw emotional energy and reinvest it in another relationship. The first two tasks in Worden's scheme put the grief work hypothesis into practice, and the last two tasks identify what bereavement resolution amounts to.

Worden has twice revised the fourth task and once the second. Now the second task reads "to process the pain of grief" (Worden, 2009). Worden initially revised the fourth task, apparently in response to empirical data on continuing bonds that emphasized that individuals often retained an internalized tie with the deceased person, to read "To emotionally relocate the deceased and move on with life." He kept this new wording until 2009 when he changed it to read even more as an endorsement of continuing bonds: "To find an enduring connection with the deceased in the midst of embarking on a new life."

Closely related to Worden's approach and clearly accepting the grief work hypothesis are the three tasks of bereavement resolution that Parkes and Weiss (1983) devised. These tasks are: intellectual acceptance of the loss; emotional acceptance of the loss; and formation of a new sense of self. Both task models emphasize that emotional detachment and reintegrating oneself into the world are desired end products of grieving, that is, markers of bereavement resolution.

Kübler-Ross and Five Stages of Grieving

In 1969 Kübler-Ross published *On Death and Dying*, in which she wrote of her work with persons who were aware they were dying. These assertions about emotional responses to dying were quickly transformed into a popular understanding of how humans respond to any significant loss. The five stages involve denial, anger, bargaining, depression, and acceptance. Kübler-Ross enthusiastically endorsed the spread of her model to the process of grieving not only losses due to deaths but any form of irreparable loss (Kübler-Ross & Kessler, 2005).

Concerns over applications of Kübler-Ross's ideas stem from two sources.[i] One concern is that the five stages have become a normative prescription, and if a person is not following the sequence then the person is not dying or grieving properly. Emphasis on these hypothetical stages takes away from the individuality and complexity of each person who is dying or who is grieving (see Kastenbaum, 2004). When taken to be a valid account of how persons move through dying or grieving, Kübler-Ross's description of five stages has led counselors to concentrate on moving a person from one stage to the next. The simplicity of the model lends itself to people who cannot tolerate ambiguity or complexity and who like simple answers.

Another concern is that despite efforts to demonstrate empirically the progression through the five stages, no evidence has emerged. These research efforts have taken the notion of stages seriously and applied the criteria that must be present for a stage theory to work: the stages must be qualitatively different, they must be irreversible, they must occur in an invariant sequence, and they must be universal. To apply just one of the criteria that must be present for a stage theory to be accepted, let us look at "irreversibility." This criterion means that once a person moves from one stage to the next, there is no return to the former stage. Yet Kübler-Ross herself wrote that return to an earlier stage was not uncommon.

As far back as the 1970s, research efforts could find no empirical confirmation to support Kübler-Ross's claims of a five-stage progression toward acceptance of dying (Metzger, 1979; Schulz & Aderman, 1974). Kübler-Ross herself offered no evidence since the publication of her book in 1969, and many clinicians and scholars have criticized the five stages for being misleading, superficial, evidence-poor, and inadequate (Kastenbaum, 2004; Klass, 1982; Pattison, 1977; Shneidman, 1980).

Some research concerns about the Kübler-Ross model include the lack of operational definitions of any of the stages and lack of tests of reliability to see if other persons examining the same interviews with dying patients come to the same conclusions that Kübler-Ross claimed. Further, Kübler-Ross reported only data about individuals she said depicted the reality of a specific stage, and did not offer longitudinal data showing the progression over time of a person through the five stages. Thus there is no reliable data that dying or grieving people actually do move from denial to acceptance via anger, bargaining, and depression. Kübler-Ross presented clinical snapshots of an individual in a specific stage, but never any evidence showing a person passing through all five stages. While retaining a remarkable hold on the popular imagination, as well as on some clinicians and teachers, Kübler-Ross's five stages of dying (and of grieving) have been jettisoned by persons in thanatology. The lasting power of the model in popular culture is likely due to its simplicity and its giving names to complicated and at times perplexing experiences with loss. Despite any misgivings about the validity or reliability of the stages, skeptics can at least agree that the five-stage model depicts resolution or recovery as the culmination or end product of acceptance. However, the means whereby a person moves from one stage to another is unspecified. An irony is that the criticism of linearity would be leveled at Kübler-Ross had she been consistent in the assumptions of stage theories; however, she violates a major tenet of stage theories, namely, she acknowledges people can and do return to earlier stages.

Recent Conceptual and Empirical Challenges to Grief Work

A variety of scholarly approaches since the early 1990s has concluded that the grief work hypothesis, including its depiction in Kübler-Ross's five-stage model, is questionable. Much of this research has focused on the resolution of grief (Archer, 1999, 2008). The following sections will focus on some of the most important contributions to our current thinking about how responses to human bereavement occur, in particular, a cognitive framework to understand coping with bereavement.

Trajectories of Bereavement

Longitudinal research with large databases has uncovered three common outcomes to bereavement over time (see particularly Bonanno, 2009; Bonanno, Boerner, & Wortman, 2008). The outcomes are three trajectories:

- A *resiliency trajectory*, comprising the plurality and at times the majority of persons studied. This trajectory is marked by initial distress over the death but return within a few weeks to normal functioning. Persons in a resiliency trajectory have not had their assumptive worlds challenged, nor is there any suggestion that they grappled with grief work, including moving through the Kübler-Ross stages.
- A *recovery trajectory*, comprising around 40% or a bit more of persons grieving the death of a loved one. This trajectory is marked by ongoing distress that gradually dissipates within 18–24 months, but has marked recurrences of grief until the person finally returns to normal functioning. This trajectory can be examined for the presence of ongoing grief work, but most researchers do not consider the Kübler-Ross stage model worth including as a viable candidate to explain movement toward bereavement resolution.
- An *enduring grief trajectory*, comprising approximately 10% of grievers. This trajectory is marked by ongoing acute distress that is ameliorated only with professional intervention. One earmark of persons in an enduring grief trajectory is an extensive refusal to acknowledge that the death has occurred, but evidence-based practices to work with persons in complicated bereavement do not promote moving persons from denial into the remaining stages in Kübler-Ross's model. Rather, the treatment focuses on such techniques as desensitizing the griever to trauma, examining issues of attachment, loss, and reattachment, using eye movement desensitization and reprocessing (EMDR), and engaging the person in neuroimaging about the deceased (Zhang, El-Jawahri, & Prigerson, 2006).

The grief work hypothesis has no trouble assimilating the recovery trajectory and the enduring grief trajectory. It is plausible that the grievers who sought clinical help and/or participation in bereavement research studies were struggling with bereavement, and by definition these individuals are not part of a resiliency response to bereavement. However, the fact that the plurality and perhaps the majority of bereaved individuals do not struggle for very long to re-acquire emotional and behavioral equilibrium does not falsify the grief work hypothesis. It is possible that persons in the recovery trajectory clearly fit what Freud and the followers of the grief work hypothesis have asserted: for them recovery from bereavement is an arduous process marked by confronting the distress that one's loss causes and, possibly, by openly disclosing one's grief to others.

The Dual Process Model

In the late 1990s the Dual Process Model of coping with bereavement identified naturally occurring processes in persons who were coming to terms with a death (Stroebe & Schut, 1999). One process was a focus on the loss itself and on the outcomes of that loss, and another process was reintegrating oneself back into the world of the living. The former process was termed a "loss orientation," and the latter process a "restoration orientation." Bereaved persons naturally oscillated between these two orientations.

How the dual process model challenged the grief work hypothesis and other theories such as the phases and stages and tasks of grieving was with empirical evidence, showing that people who recovered from bereavement did not continuously confront the distress of the loss. However, in itself the dual process model does not falsify the grief work hypothesis but rather discloses that prevailing understandings of grief work incompletely portray what coping with bereavement entails. A significant challenge would come if empirical data indicated it was common for most bereaved persons to spend all their time in the restoration process.

Avoidance of Distress

Some research, particularly from Bonanno and his colleagues (1995), showed an unexpected relationship between not focusing on one's distress and subsequent reductions of bereavement-related problems. That is, the less people concentrated on the distress of their bereavement, the more they showed increases in health and decreases in grief. Constantly focusing on distress, sometimes called "rumination" (Bonanno, Papa, Lalande, Zhang, & Noll, 2005; van der Houwen, Stroebe, Schut, Stroebe, & van den Bout, 2010), has been demonstrated to be counter-productive.

Archer (1999, p. 135) wrote that Bonanno's research studies question "a version of the grief work hypothesis that concentrates on the supposed value of outward expression of emotions. However, it is also apparent that the concept of grief work is not always restricted to emotional expression," but—at least in Lindemann's version of the grief work hypothesis—extends to self-disclosure of one's feelings. Wolfgang Stroebe and his colleagues (W. Stroebe, Schut, & M. Stroebe, 2005) have empirical results challenging the value of self-disclosure for recovery from bereavement; in their study, persons with high distress continued to have high distress regardless of whether they shared their feelings with other people. Refraining from disclosing the pain of one's bereavement enables grievers to maintain interpersonal contacts with persons who avoid people who continually share painful, negative feelings. Bereaved college students have stated that they learned that few, if any, peers wanted to hear about their loss; to stay in contact with these persons, it was better to keep their feelings disguised (Balk, 2011).

Yet these findings about camouflaging grief do not take into account the consistently positive accounts of the value of support groups comprised of persons who share their distress in a safe, accepting environment (Balk, Tyson-Rawson, & Colletti-Wetzel, 1993; Rich, 2002; Schuurman, 2008). As one example, bereaved college students have remarked on how much they appreciate finding one or more peers with the emotional maturity to listen attentively to a bereaved person's story (Balk, 2011).

Pennebaker's (1997; Pennebaker, Zech, Rime, 2001) long-term research program into negative life events and the personal value of disclosing to others presents another set of data cautioning against wholesale rejection of the value of self-disclosure. The more that persons grieving traumatic events, in particular homicides and suicides, disclosed their experiences, the less they engaged in obsessively thinking (that is, ruminating) on the event and the more their health improved. Disclosing extended to writing about the event, not just to telling someone else face-to-face, and was linked to physiological indicators of improved health. Archer noted that it is not just writing or talking about the event that proves helpful but rather "it is the integration and cognitive reorganization of the event that expression enables which leads to health changes" (1999, p. 136).

Constructivism

The cognitive revolution that has won the day in much of psychology has made its mark in both conceptual and empirical work on coping with bereavement. Cognitive models of coping with stressful life events have been applied to bereavement with promising results. At the heart of these cognitive models are proactive tasks identified in empirical research with persons coping with such life crises as alcoholism, diabetes, divorce, and bereavement. The tasks include establishing the personal significance of the event, maintaining interpersonal relationships, confronting the demands of the event, regulating emotional expression, and preserving a sense of self-efficacy. A representative example of this cognitive approach is the coping model devised by Moos and Schaefer (1986) and applied in a longitudinal intervention with bereaved college students (Balk, Tyson-Rawson, & Colletti-Wetzel, 1993).

Fulfilling the tasks is seen to be non-linear in that new life events will occasion revisiting a task previously accomplished. An 11-year-old daughter coping with the death of her father will revisit that event and the personal significance of her father's death when she reaches various developmental milestones such as graduating from high school, getting married, and giving birth.

Building on the seminal work of Kelly (1955), Neimeyer has developed a cognitive model based primarily if not solely in the task of meaning making (Neimeyer, 2001). The crux of the issue for bereavement resolution in Neimeyer's model is to establish the meaning of one's bereavement. This process of constructing meaning involves three interrelated activities: sense making, benefit finding, and identity change. All three activities point both to how persons resolve bereavement and what bereavement resolution consists of.

Continuing Bonds

While it may not have inaugurated the skepticism about whether grief work works, the idea of continuing bonds presented a specific denunciation of a central component in the grief work hypothesis. That central component is the equation of bereavement resolution with emotional detachment from the person who died.

Primacy for the discovery of continuing bonds typically goes to Dennis Klass, Phyllis Silverman, and Steven Nickman (1996). However, other scholars, in particular Nancy Hogan, had also been informing us about ongoing attachments reported by bereaved adolescent siblings (Hogan & DeSantis, 1992).

No idea in thanatology has so quickly been championed as has the notion of continuing bonds. Initially, continuing bonds was presented as a needed corrective to the sweeping generalization that bereavement resolution requires emotionally detaching from the deceased. As Klass noted in his study of bereaved parents (1988), they had confronted the distress of their children's deaths and were functioning well in society, but among themselves they shared a secret they would not tell to outsiders: they remained emotionally attached to their dead child. The clinical mainstream said it was pathological to remain attached, but here were well-functioning bereaved adults who refused to accept what the mainstream said was abnormal.

Continuing bonds does present a major challenge to the grief work hypothesis. A principal indicator of successful grieving has been cast aside; there has not been repudiation of the necessity of confronting the distress that the child's death evokes. However, that point seems to have been overlooked in wholesale acceptance of continuing bonds as the new norm. Whereas before a person was considered pathological for maintaining an emotional bond with the deceased, soon the prescription was emerging that a continuing bond was expected, and the implication was that it was pathological for there not to be a continuing bond. Empirical research looking at attachment styles and ongoing attachments have clarified that continuing bonds are healthy when there was a secure attachment established prior to the death, but loosening of these attachment bonds is recommended when attachment bonds were insecure (Archer, 2008; M. Stroebe, Schut, & Stroebe, 2003). In addition, some widows have publicly acknowledged that the deaths of their husbands had been liberating, not losses leading to ongoing attachments, because the husbands had been oppressive and abusive (Elison & McGonigle, 2003).

Closing Comments

In this chapter I have looked at various ideas offered for explaining how bereaved persons adapt to loss. The initial impetus for writing the chapter was to address the loss of support for stage-based and phase-based models as viable explanations for coping with bereavement. It struck me that the issue would best be dealt with by framing the matter in light of grief work theory and the alternatives to it that have emerged, particularly since the 1990s. Here there has been an increased affirmation that any models of the grieving process need to acknowledge the many individual pathways as persons cope with loss.

---

[1] A new source of radical skepticism about Kübler-Ross can be found in Konigsberg's (2011) portrait of Kübler-Ross. Konigsberg raises serious questions about Kübler-Ross's methodology as well as the originality of her stage theory.

David E. Balk *is a professor at Brooklyn College where he directs graduate studies in Thanatology. He earned a BA in philosophy from Immaculate Conception Seminary, an MA in theology from Marquette University, an MC in counselor education from Arizona State University, and a PhD in counseling psychology from the University of Illinois at Urbana-Champaign. He is the author of the book* Helping the Bereaved College Student, *published in 2011 by Springer Publishing Company. Dr. Balk is a member of the Association for Death Education and Counseling (ADEC), and chaired ADEC's Scientific Advisory Committee from 2008–2011. He is the book review editor for* Death Studies, *and is a member of the editorial board of* Omega: Journal of Death and Dying.

REFERENCES

Archer, J. (1999). *The nature of grief: The evolution and psychology of reactions to loss.* London: Routledge.

Archer, J. (2008). Theories of grief: Past, present, and future perspectives. In M. S. Stroebe, R. O. Hansson, H. Schut, & W. Stroebe (Eds.), *Handbook of bereavement research and practice: Advances in theory and intervention* (pp. 45–65). Washington, DC: American Psychological Association.

Balk, D. E. (Editor). (2008). Bereavement, outcomes, and recovery. Special issue. *Death Studies, 32*(1).

Balk, D. E. (2011). *Helping the bereaved college student.* New York: Springer Publishing Company.

Balk, D. E., Tyson-Rawson, K., & Colletti-Wetzel, J. (1993). Social support as an intervention with bereaved college students. *Death Studies, 17,* 427–450.

Bonanno, G. A. (2009). *The other side of sadness: What the new science of bereavement tells us about life after loss.* New York: Basic Books.

Bonanno, G. A., Boerner, K., & Wortman, C. B. (2008). Trajectories of grieving. In M. S. Stroebe, R. O. Hansson, H. Schut, & W. Stroebe (Eds.), *Handbook of bereavement research and practice: Advances in theory and intervention* (pp. 287–307). Washington, DC: American Psychological Association.

Bonanno, G. A., Keltner, D., Holen, A., & Horowitz, M. J. (1995). When avoiding unpleasant emotions might not be a bad thing: Verbal autonomic response dissociation and midlife conjugal bereavement. *Journal of Personality and Social Psychology, 69,* 975–989.

Bonanno, G. A., Papa. A., Lalande, K., Zhang, N., & Noll, J. G. (2005). Grief processing and deliberate grief avoidance: A prospective comparison of bereaved spouses and parents in the United States and the People's Republic of China. *Journal of Counseling and Clinical Psychology, 73,* 86–98.

Bowlby, J. (1969–1980). *Attachment and loss.* New York: Basic Books. [Vol, 1, *Attachment;* Vol. 2, *Separation: Anxiety and anger;* Vol. 3, *Loss: Sadness and depression.*]

Cook, A. S., & Oltjenbruns, K. A. (1989). *Dying and grieving: Lifespan and family perspectives.* New York: Holt, Rinehart, and Winston.

Elison, J., & McGonigle, C. (2003). *Liberating losses: When death brings relief.* Cambridge, MA: Perseus.

Freud, S. (1957). Mourning and melancholia. In J. Strachey (Ed. & Trans.), *The standard edition of the complete psychological works of Sigmund Freud* (vol. 14, pp. 243–258). London: Hogarth Press. (Original work published 1917.)

Gillies, J., & Neimeyer, R. A. (2006). Loss, grief, and the search for significance: Toward a model of meaning reconstruction in bereavement. *Journal of Constructivist Psychology, 19,* 31–65.

Hogan, N., & DeSantis, L. (1992). Adolescent sibling bereavement: An ongoing attachment. *Qualitative Health Research, 2*(2), 159–177.

Kastenbaum, R. (2004). *Death, society, and human experience* (8th ed.). Boston: Allyn & Bacon.

Kelly, G. A. (1955). *The psychology of personal constructs.* Volume 1. New York: Norton.

Klass, D. (1982). Elisabeth Kübler-Ross and the tradition of the private sphere: An analysis of symbols. *Omega: Journal of Death and Dying, 12,* 241–261.

Klass, D. (1988). *Parental grief: Solace and resolution.* New York: Springer Publishing.

Klass, D., Silverman, P. R., & Nickman, S. L. (1996). (Eds.). *Continuing bonds: New understandings of grief.* Philadelphia: Taylor & Francis.

Konigsberg, R. D. (2011). *The truth about grief: The myth of its five stages and the new science of loss.* New York: Simon & Schuster.

Kübler-Ross, E. (1969). *On death and dying.* New York: Macmillan.

Kübler-Ross, E., & Kessler, D. (2005). *On grief and grieving: Finding the meaning of grief through the five stages of loss.* New York: Scribners.

Lindemann, E. (1944). The symptomatology and management of acute grief. *American Journal of Psychiatry, 101,* 141–148.

Metzger, A. M. (1979). A Q-methodological study of the Kübler-Ross stage theory. *Omega: Journal of Death and Dying, 10,* 291–302.

Moos, R. H., & Schaefer, J. A. (1986). Life transitions and crises: A conceptual overview. *Coping with life crises: An integrated approach* (pp. 3–28). New York: Plenum.

Neimeyer, R. A. (Ed.). (2001). *Meaning reconstruction and the experience of loss.* Washington, DC: American Psychological Association.

Parkes, C. M., & Weiss, R. (1983). *Recovery from bereavement.* New York: Basic Books.

Pattison, E. M. (1977). *The experience of dying.* Englewood, NJ: Prentice-Hall.

Pennebaker, J. W. (1997). Writing about emotional experiences as a therapeutic process. *Psychological Science, 8,* 162–166.

Pennebaker, J. W., Zech, E., & Rime, B. (2001). Disclosing and sharing emotions: Psychological, social and health consequences. In M. S. Stroebe, W. Stroebe, R. O. Hansson, & H. Schut (Eds.), *Handbook of bereavement research: Consequences, coping and care* (pp. 517–543). Washington DC: American Psychological Association.

Rich, M. D. (2002). Memory Circles: The implications of (not) grieving at cancer camps. *Journal of Contemporary Ethnography, 31,* 548–581.

Schulz, R., & Aderman, D. (1974). Clinical research and the stages of dying. *Omega: Journal of Death and Dying, 3,* 137–144.

Schuurman, D. (2008). Grief groups for grieving children and adolescents. In K. J. Doka & A. S. Tucci (Eds.), *Living with grief: Children and adolescents* (pp. 255–268). Washington, DC: Hospice Foundation of America.

Shneidman, E. S. (1980). *Voices of death.* New York: Harper & Row.

Stroebe, M., & Schut, H. (1999). The dual process model of coping with bereavement: Rationale and description. *Death Studies, 23,* 197–224.

Stroebe, M., Schut, H., & Boerner, K. (2010). Continuing bonds in adaptation to bereavement: Toward theoretical integration. *Clinical Psychology Review, 30,* 259–268.

Stroebe, M. S., Schut, H., & Stroebe, W. (2003). Attachment in coping with bereavement: A theoretical perspective. *Review of General Psychology, 9,* 48–66.

Stroebe, W., Schut, H., & Stroebe, M. S. (2005). Grief work, disclosure, and counseling: Do they help the bereaved? *Clinical Psychology Review, 25,* 395–414.

van der Houwen, K., Stroebe, M., Schut, H., Stroebe, W., & van den Bout, J. (2010). Mediating processes in bereavement: The role of rumination, threatening grief interpretations, and deliberate grief avoidance. *Social Science & Medicine, 71,* 1669–1676.

Worden, J. W. (2009). *Grief counseling and grief therapy: A handbook for the mental health practitioner* (4th ed.). New York: Springer Publishing Company.

Zhang, B., El-Jawahri, A., & Prigerson, H. G. (2006). Update on bereavement research: Evidence-based guidelines for the diagnosis and treatment of complicated bereavement. *Journal of Palliative Medicine, 9,* 1188–1203.

CHAPTER 5

Positive Transformations in Response to the Struggle With Grief

Richard G. Tedeschi, Lawrence G. Calhoun, and Elizabeth Addington

Although the loss of a loved one is difficult under any circumstances, it may be most difficult when there is no sense of meaning to the loss (Keesee, Currier, & Neimeyer, 2008). People who feel that their loved one died in vain or that the death was senseless may have a more difficult path than those who see some redeeming aspect to the loss. Some of these redemptive aspects might be that the loved one died for an important cause or doing what he or she loved, or that the death was part of God's plan.

Another possible outcome in grief is positive transformation in the aftermath of the struggle with the loss (Calhoun & Tedeschi, 1989–1990). There has been a growing recognition of this possibility among professionals who serve the bereaved (Bonanno & Mancini, 2008; Hogan & Schmidt, 2002; Kessler, 1987; Nerken, 1993; Tedeschi & Calhoun, 2004b; Znoj, 2006). We coined the term "posttraumatic growth" (Tedeschi & Calhoun, 1996) to describe positive transformations that people can experience as they cope with grief and other highly stressful life circumstances (Calhoun & Tedeschi, 1999). As we have elsewhere, we use the words *traumatic* and *posttraumatic* to mean something broader than the very restricted definitions in the current *Diagnostic and Statistical Manual of Mental Disorders* (American Psychiatric Association, 2000). The words are used here interchangeably with the terms *life crisis, major stressor,* and *highly stressful event* to refer to life circumstances that severely challenge people's adaptive resources, particularly their general ways of understanding the world and their place in it. Our focus in this chapter is on the answer to this question: What kinds of positive transformations can emerge from one's struggle with grief, and how does this happen? We will also offer some thoughts on how clinicians can approach the possibilities of growth with their grieving clients.

When a child dies, for example, parents typically face intense suffering and anguish, the possibility of significant impairment in major social roles, and a grieving process that may be protracted and distressing (Hazzard, Weston, & Gutteres, 1992; Oliver, 1999; Romanoff, 1993; Rubin & Malkinson, 2001). Almost paradoxically, however, some persons who experience the death of a loved one also report significant psychological growth emerging from their struggle with major loss (Calhoun, Tedeschi, Cann, & Hanks, 2010; Lehman et al., 1993; Talbot, 1998–1999; Tedeschi & Calhoun, 2004b).

Domains of Positive Transformation

Consider the words of some bereaved parents with whom we have worked and who were participants in our research. These statements reflect the five dimensions of posttraumatic growth that we have uncovered empirically (Taku, Cann, Calhoun, & Tedeschi, 2008; Tedeschi & Calhoun, 1996).

> *With my husband, it has not affected [our relationship] at all adversely. I'd say that it has probably made it even stronger because he's been so supportive.*

> *We realize that life is precious and that we don't take each other for granted. In fact, my daughter in Raleigh, I talk to her almost every day on the phone, and I've found I've become much more protective than I've been before. And I'm also very much more generous with her than I have been with her previously.*

These statements refer to positive changes in ways of relating to others. Very difficult situations can strain and sometimes break relationships, but sometimes people develop deeper emotional connections with others as a result of having to deal with trauma and loss. Relationships can be strengthened for a number of reasons. People are often compelled after traumatic losses to seek out others who will listen to their story. The experience of intimacy that comes from the disclosure of such emotional experiences can produce an appreciation for relationships and a comfort with intimacy that was not previously felt. The greater sense of closeness may go beyond connections with significant others to include an enhanced sense of connectedness to other human beings in general and particularly to people who suffer, especially those who have undergone or are undergoing a similar kind of suffering. It is not yet clear whether this increased feeling of being connected and wanting to comfort others who have experienced a similar loss results in a general tendency toward greater altruism

(Staub & Vollhardt, 2008). But certainly the sense of increased psychological connectedness to other human beings appears to be present.

Grieving persons may also experience positive transformation in the form of a new understanding of themselves as stronger or more capable (Janoff-Bulman, 2006).

> *The main thing is the strength. The understanding that God is going to get you through anything that happens to you. And that gives you a different outlook on life. That gives you a different view of how to handle things. That takes away a lot of the fear and trepidation that most of us walk through life with. That doesn't mean I don't have any fear or that I don't think about the future or any of that stuff. I do, just like normal people. But I'm not constantly worried about it.*
>
> *I've been through the absolute worst that I know. And no matter what happens, I'll be able to deal with it.*

Dealing with a crisis can provide a new recognition of one's personal strength. After a highly stressful event, it may be hard to imagine that anything worse could happen, and people may conclude that no other event can overtax their coping abilities. This may be true; however, people can encounter a terrible "pileup" of traumas that overwhelm them and make growth less likely (Harvey, Barnett, & Rupe, 2006).

> *I think that you become conscious of the fact that every day is a new day; a beginning or a possible ending.... I have always appreciated what I have, but I just think you have a greater appreciation for things that are there that maybe you have experienced and shared with that child that you lost.*

These statements reflect the increased appreciation of life that can come with severe losses. Losing something precious can demonstrate that one should appreciate what one has. Strikingly, many people who report this type of posttraumatic growth mention their newfound appreciation for rather ordinary, everyday living. This suggests a shift in the perception of what is truly valuable, a shift in priorities regarding how one should spend time and effort.

> I've become very empathic toward anybody in pain or in any kind of grief. I think that's one reason I went into oncology nursing—because I felt so comfortable around grief. And I felt very comfortable around death and dying because I've learned so much about it and love talking about it.

Some people strike out on new life ventures or pathways in the aftermath of loss. This may be related to the other dimensions of posttraumatic growth. For example, finding the value in relationships may move a person toward service to others and appreciating life more profoundly may produce a shift toward activities that embrace experiences that seem simple but are now more vividly felt.

> I have had to work out my relationship with God. For a while, I wasn't sure I had one anymore. But in the end, I think I have a deeper understanding of things like grace, and I think I have had to really figure out how to be forgiving, too.

Another domain in which bereaved persons can experience growth is in spiritual, religious, or existential matters. The trajectories and content of change vary greatly, but the central theme is a change in one's general philosophy of life that leads to a philosophy with which one is more satisfied. Persons who struggle with significant loss do not necessarily become more religious or spiritual. For some, this is the case; for others, the change is to a more satisfying but perhaps less orthodox stance. The death of a loved one raises existential questions for some bereaved persons and growth may be reflected in a greater satisfaction with one's religious or spiritual views but not necessarily a greater adherence to particular beliefs or practices.

How Do Transformations Occur?

A substantial body of literature describes the transformations people report in the aftermath of loss. But exactly how are people transformed by their grief? (See Calhoun, Cann, & Tedeschi, 2010; Calhoun & Tedeschi, 2004, 2006; and Tedeschi & Calhoun, 1995, 2004a for fuller descriptions of the hypothesized process.) To understand this transformation, it may be useful to see the loss of a loved one as a major life crisis.

For many people, a major life crisis triggers a series of difficult cognitive and emotional adjustments that are necessary to make sense of the loss. These attempts to adjust can set the stage for growth. In our description of this process

(Calhoun & Tedeschi, 2006), we draw on the work of Janoff-Bulman (1992, 2006), who in turn uses Parkes's (1971) conception of the role of assumptive worlds and Epstein's (1990) ideas about the individual's "world-theory" to guide expectations about the life course.

Significant losses can challenge—and perhaps shatter—these expectations or assumptions, and require people to rethink them (Cann et al., 2010a). The assumptions tend to be general assumptions (such as views on the nature of human beings, good and evil, and the workings of the universe) and specific assumptions (such as predictions about how vulnerable one is to tragedy, how benevolent the world is, and what the future holds). Losses that are particularly unexpected or that go against the "normal" course of events, such as the death of a child, are most likely to set in motion the questioning and reconsideration that may eventually allow the person once again to think of the world as understandable or predictable. This process can take years. Losses that seem unbelievable long after they have occurred are particular challenges to the assumptive world.

Another way to consider this process of transformation is to approach it from the standpoint of constructivist and narrative psychology (Neimeyer, 2006; Neimeyer, Burke, Mackay, & van Dyke Stringer, 2010). If we think of people as semi-deliberately engaged in a process of creating their own autobiographies, losses can be seen as discontinuities in their life stories. These surprising and unwanted intrusions demand a change in the story. If a loss is going to be transformative, it will be highly disruptive to the ongoing story, which has a planned and assumed structure. People often describe these losses later in terms of "before" and "after"—they are the turning points in their lives. Life has been transformed by the intrusion of death. It cannot proceed as it was; the person's life story has been permanently changed.

The transformations that occur as a result of the struggle with loss are sometimes for the better and sometimes for the worse, although they are not usually an either/or proposition. Both positive and negative consequences are part of the story, as disruption sets into motion the questioning of the assumptive world—the predictions made about how life will go and what kind of person one will be. It is important to underscore what for clinicians may be an obvious point—posttraumatic growth will probably not eliminate distress. However, it may allow the loss to be somewhat better tolerated, because the loss and the suffering have not been in vain. If the struggle with loss produces something meaningful, it can be honored and not merely endured.

Another factor that may be important in the process of transforming grief is the kind and quality of the social responses grieving persons receive, especially from those closest to them (Calhoun, Cann, & Tedeschi, 2010; Calhoun & Tedeschi, 2006). In response to trauma, some people want to tell the story of what happened—the events and their aftermath. Some people may need to retell the story of their loss, perhaps many times, before they are able to accept the outcomes. Friends and family may need to have patience with the grieving person. If they are unwilling or uncomfortable listening, and, therefore, put constraints on the person who is attempting to describe his or her grief and bereavement, that person may have even more difficulty coming to terms with the loss. Researchers and clinicians are only beginning to understand how social outlets for expressions of grief are changing with the growing use of online communities (van der Houwen et al., 2010; Vicary & Fraley, 2010). Nonetheless, it appears that the cognitive and emotional processing often necessary in the aftermath of a major loss can be helped or hindered by the responses of others (Calhoun, Cann, & Tedeschi, 2010; Taku, Tedeschi, Cann, & Calhoun, 2009). Positive transformations may hinge on the extent to which the grieving person receives support or suffers from social constraints against talking about the loss generally (Lepore, Silver, Wortman, & Wayment, 1996) and the experience of transformation in particular.

What does social constraint look like? How is it experienced by the grieving person? Constraints on disclosure and the negative responses of others to disclosure can lead to feelings that the process is taking too long, that the emotions need to be cut short or put away, or that the person or the story is to be avoided. Such responses are hurtful to bereaved persons, who may tend to adopt the view of those who impose the constraints. Grieving persons in such social contexts may come to question the appropriateness of their thoughts, feelings, and behavior. They may worry that they are not grieving in "healthy" ways, or they may feel pressure to "get over it." An antidote to this situation that can enable more adaptive processing of the loss is what we call "expert companionship" (Tedeschi & Calhoun, 2004b; Tedeschi & Calhoun, 2010). Cognitive processing of loss into growth experiences can occur when listeners are sensitive, courageous, and patient, and respect the bereaved person's ways of coming to terms with the loss.

How to Assist: The Expert Companion

Although it is currently enjoying great interest and popularity (justifiably so), the idea that clinicians need to understand their clients in the context of specific cultural contexts is not new at all (e.g., Kanfer & Saslow, 1969). We have addressed the importance of understanding clients in their own unique socio-cultural contexts in more detail elsewhere (Calhoun, Cann, & Tedeschi, 2010; Calhoun & Tedeschi, 2004, 2006; Tedeschi & Calhoun, 2004a), and research has shown that posttraumatic growth occurs in a wide range of cultural settings (Weiss & Berger, 2010). Still, it may be useful to make some recommendations here about the grieving person's socio-cultural context.

All of us are members of social and cultural groups that range from geographically and interpersonally close, usually small, communities (a gang, a team, a family), to much larger and somewhat more abstract social entities (a nationality, an ethnic group). The groups to which we belong provide cues on how we should behave and sometimes provide feedback on the desirability or undesirability of our behavior. The most important feedback comes from the people in the groups with whom we regularly interact, though our beliefs can also be informed by the larger groups with which we identify. This is clearly the case for grief and bereavement: Different social groups have different rules about how, when, and where mourning rituals should unfold; appropriate and inappropriate ways to understand and cope with loss; and how people should express their experience and emotions. What follows must be considered in light of the wide array of social and cultural prisms through which individuals experience bereavement.

The clinician who wishes to assist bereaved persons should be a companion and equal first, but also must have expertise (Tedeschi & Calhoun, 2004b). Bereaved persons who seek professional help may need *expert companions* to help them manage significant emotional distress, reconsider and perhaps disengage from goals that are no longer attainable, and rework their life narratives. This process can be a lengthy one. Expert companions can tolerate the sometimes slow process of reconsidering the assumptive world, constructing a new version that accommodates the loss, and dealing with subsequent difficulties.

It is important to note that although our focus here is on helping bereaved persons who have sought professional help with their grief or who appear to be having significant difficulties adapting to their loss, most people who lose a loved one do not require or seek professional help (Bonanno & Mancini, 2008; Tedeschi & Calhoun, 2004b; Wortman & Silver, 1989). We believe that most grieving persons appreciate and are probably helped by the socially intelligent support provided by the various communities and social groups to which they belong—extended families, friends, and members of social communities—but most people neither want nor need professional mental health interventions designed to address "grief issues."

Although our audience here consists primarily of professionals whose work puts them in regular contact with dying or bereaved persons, the following recommendations can also provide a useful framework for those who offer informal support for grieving friends and relatives. The following suggestions can be used to help grieving persons survive a loss and to acknowledge any posttraumatic growth they may have experienced.

Throughout the process, it is important to recognize that the transformations of grief are essentially paradoxical. The fundamental paradox is that loss can produce gain. There are other paradoxes as well: Grieving involved oscillation between attempts to restore life and engagement in the emotional tasks of mourning the loss (Stroebe & Schut, 1999); grieving involves re-forming one's relationship to the loved one who has died (Neimeyer, 2010); and support from others is important, even though the loss is a painfully personal and sometimes lonely situation. The more substantial the grieving person's coping abilities, the more successful he or she will be at engaging in these processes. Znoj (2006) describes how adaptive coping—especially good emotional regulation, the ability to accept tragic situations, and the use of (rather than abuse of) available supports—is crucial to this process. The expert companion may be able to use these approaches to help people, even those who do not have the best coping abilities, find their way through grief to personal transformation.

In a form of support that is based primarily on companionship, several elements can facilitate posttraumatic growth. The message given by the expert companion is that grieving persons can be trusted to find their way through the grief. Grieving is an individual journey; it does not follow one set of steps or involve certain universal responses. Trusting clients with the process of grief honors their personal strength, even when they may doubt it themselves. This provides an important building block for developing the enhanced sense of personal strength that many people report as an aspect of posttraumatic growth.

The expert companion can model and nurture closer relationships with others. This kind of companionship is based on a type of listening that allows the listener—that is, the expert companion—also to be changed, rather than focusing on changing the client. This open attitude toward listening can encourage a deeper exploration of feelings and a level of trust in a relationship that may never have been possible before. The devastation of grief can leave people emotionally raw and much less able to manage their impressions and contain their tears. Responding to this raw emotion with expert companionship can produce a new depth of relating.

Among the many issues that may concern grieving persons who seek help are spiritual and existential questions, and dilemmas about the life course. Expert companions must be comfortable discussing questions with existential, spiritual and sometimes religious content that touch on, for example, the extent to which God controls events and whether comfort can be found in the spiritual life. The loss of a close relationship can also alter the life course, bringing new roles and new responsibilities.

Many people in grief are understandably reluctant to acknowledge any positive consequences of their struggle with loss. Clients who are desperately missing a loved one might mistake recognition of growth for a suggestion that the death was in some way fortunate. The expert companion takes the view that it is not the loss itself that has value, but the *struggle* with that loss that can be transformative. Losses can be mourned even as positive changes become evident. At the appropriate time and in the appropriate context, the expert companion judiciously helps the client acknowledge and accept the positive transformations that have occurred.

While some people are reluctant to acknowledge growth in the aftermath of grief, others embrace it as a way of honoring the loved one who has died. They may take responsibility for carrying on the person's work or keeping his or her memory alive, which may take them to places in life that they never anticipated. The bereaved parent quoted above who became an oncology nurse did so in part to honor the memory of the child she lost to cancer. These new possibilities are one of the domains of posttraumatic growth and may be the most unambiguous indications of growth.

The expert companion can encourage clients as they begin to move into new territory. For example, a widow was faced with a decision about what to do with her husband's business. She had always been a homemaker, but she had discussed the business with her husband for years and knew most of the employees. She decided to run it herself and was surprised at her ability and the joy she found in the work. At first, she felt that she was preserving what he had built rather than letting it die with him, but over time she expanded and improved the business, putting her own stamp on the endeavor. She could take pride in her accomplishments and honor her husband as well. This path also allowed her to channel her grief into productive activity.

Conclusions

Although it is clear that grief can be a transformative event, those who work with grieving persons should be careful not to judge outcomes by the presence or absence of such changes. Grief can take a longer course than was assumed in the past, and transformations may take longer as well. Where a client is at one point in time may not be indicative of the reactions he or she will show later in the process. It is also important to recognize the complicated relationship between resolution of grief and posttraumatic growth. For example, bereaved parents may experience ongoing distress related to posttraumatic growth, and parents who say they have resolved their grief may be less likely to see anything good as having come out of their struggle with the loss of a child (Znoj, 2006).

The view that positive transformation can coexist with suffering, or that ongoing distress may serve as the impetus for growth, tends not to fit well with the general assumptions of many North American clinicians. A pervasive way of thinking about growth seems to go like this: Growth is positive, and positive psychological outcomes mean that the person is happy and not distressed; therefore, growth should be associated with more positive psychological outcomes and fewer negative outcomes. The findings that growth and distress tend to be independent do not easily fit into the general framework of some clinicians and researchers.

We are not suggesting that a therapeutic goal of enhanced client happiness is undesirable. We are suggesting, however, that the almost intuitive assumption that growth must be correlated with more happiness and less sadness is incorrect (Cann, Calhoun, Tedeschi, & Solomon, 2010). This reminder is particularly important for clinicians who work with people who are grieving an upcoming loss (as in hospice care) or the death of a loved one.

The available data do not permit a definite conclusion about the relationships among posttraumatic growth, well-being, and distress. But the data are quite clear that growth and psychological distress tend not to be related in the way we might assume. Our own view, based on current research findings, as well as our clinical work (and we are fully aware of the danger of relying on such limited and subjective data), is that some degree of ongoing psychological discomfort may ensure the maintenance of the positive transformations that can arise from the struggle with grief.

Whether continued discomfort is necessary for continued growth, it is clear that even in the midst of great suffering, a person can, at the same time, experience significant growth. Clinicians who work with grieving persons should not assume that themes of growth in the client's narrative mean that the pain of grief has been commensurately abated. But the presence of growth may be an indicator that the client is experiencing positive transformations that may make the suffering more bearable, even if it is not diminished. Both expert companions and those they are trying to serve may need to remember the words of the old Protestant hymn: *Shun not the struggle—'tis God's gift.*

Editor's Note: This chapter was revised from Tedeschi, R. G. and Calhoun, L. G., (2007). Grief as a transformative struggle. In K.J. Doka (Ed.), *Living with grief: Before and after the death,* Washington, DC: Hospice Foundation of America.

Richard G. Tedeschi *is professor of psychology at the University of North Carolina (UNC) Charlotte. Together with Dr. Calhoun, he is the originator of the term 'posttraumatic growth' and has published many works in this area. He also is a practicing clinician who has provided support group experiences for bereaved parents for over two decades.*

Lawrence G. Calhoun *is professor of psychology at UNC Charlotte. He has published numerous books and articles in the area of suicide, bereavement, trauma and posttraumatic growth during his career. He is also a recipient of university and state teaching awards.*

Elizabeth Addington *completed her BA in psychology at Wake Forest University and is currently a student in the clinical track of the Health Psychology PhD program at UNC Charlotte. Her research and clinical interests involve posttraumatic growth, coping with loss, and psycho-oncology.*

REFERENCES

American Psychiatric Association. (2000). *Diagnostic and statistical manual of mental disorders.* (Revised 4th ed.). Washington, DC: Author.

Bonanno, G. A., & Mancini, A. D. (2008). The human capacity to thrive in the face of potential trauma. *Pediatrics, 121*(2), 369–375. doi:10.1542/peds.2007-1648

Calhoun, L. G., Cann, A., & Tedeschi, R. G. (2010). The Posttraumatic Growth model: Socio-cultural considerations. In T. Weiss & R. Berger (Eds.), *Posttraumatic growth and culturally competent practice: Lessons learned from around the globe.* New York: Wiley.

Calhoun, L. G., & Tedeschi, R. G. (1989–1990). Positive aspects of critical life problems: Recollections of grief. *Omega: Journal of Death and Dying, 29,* 265–272.

Calhoun, L. G., & Tedeschi, R. G. (1999). *Facilitating posttraumatic growth: A clinician's guide.* Mahwah, NJ: Lawrence Erlbaum Associates.

Calhoun, L. G., & Tedeschi, R. G. (2004). The foundations of posttraumatic growth: New considerations. *Psychological Inquiry, 15,* 93–102.

Calhoun, L. G., & Tedeschi, R. G. (2006). The foundations of posttraumatic growth: An expanded framework. In L. G. Calhoun & R. G. Tedeschi (Eds.), *Handbook of posttraumatic growth: Research and practice* (pp. 1–23). Mahwah, NJ: Lawrence Erlbaum Associates.

Calhoun, L. G., Tedeschi, R. G., Cann, A., & Hanks, E. A. (2010). Positive outcomes following bereavement: Paths to posttraumatic growth. *Psychologica Belgica, 50*(1–2), 125–143.

Cann, A., Calhoun, L. G., Tedeschi, R. G., Kilmer, R. P., Gil-Rivas, V., Vishnevsky, T., & Danhauer, S.C. (2010a). The Core Beliefs Inventory: A brief measure of disruption in the assumptive world. *Anxiety, Stress, & Coping, 23,* 19–34.

Cann, A., Calhoun, L. G., Tedeschi, R. G., & Solomon, D. T. (2010). Posttraumatic growth and depreciation as independent experiences and predictors of well-being. *Journal of Loss and Trauma, 15*(3), 151–166. doi:10.1080/15325020903375826

Epstein, S. (1990). The self-concept, the traumatic neurosis, and the structure of personality. In D. J. Ozer, J. M. Healy, & A. J. Stewart (Eds.), *Perspectives in personality: Vol 3* (pp. 63–98). London: Jessica Kingsley.

Harvey, J., Barnett, K., & Rupe, S. (2006). Posttraumatic growth and other outcomes of major loss in the context of complex family lives. In L. G. Calhoun & R. G. Tedeschi (Eds.), *Handbook of posttraumatic growth: Research and practice* (pp. 100–117). Mahwah, NJ: Lawrence Erlbaum Associates.

Hazzard, A., Weston, J., & Guterres, C. (1992). After a child's death: Factors related to parental bereavement. *Journal of Developmental and Behavioral Pediatrics, 13,* 24–30.

Hogan, N. S., & Schmidt, L. A. (2002). Testing the grief to personal growth model using structural equation modeling. *Death Studies, 26,* 615–634.

Janoff-Bulman, R. (1992). *Shattered assumptions: Toward a new psychology of trauma.* New York: Free Press.

Janoff-Bulman, R. (2006). Schema-change perspectives on posttraumatic growth. In L. G. Calhoun & R. G. Tedeschi (Eds.), *Handbook of posttraumatic growth: Research and practice* (pp. 81–99). Mahwah, NJ: Lawrence Erlbaum Associates.

Kanfer, F. H., & Saslow, G. (1969). Behavioral diagnosis. In C. M. Franks (Ed.), *Behavior therapy—Appraisal and status* (pp. 417–444). New York: McGraw-Hill Book Co.

Keesee, N. J., Currier, J. M., & Neimeyer, R. A. (2008). Predictors of grief following the death of one's child: The contribution of finding meaning. *Journal of Clinical Psychology, 64*(10), 1145–1163. doi:10.1002/jclp.20502

Kessler, B. G. (1987). Bereavement and personal growth. *Journal of Humanistic Psychology, 27,* 228–247.

Lehman, D. R., Davis, C. G., DeLongis, A., Wortman, C. B., Bluck, S., Mandel, D., & Ellard, J. H. (1993). Positive and negative life changes following bereavement and their relations to adjustment. *Journal of Personality and Social Psychology, 12,* 90–112.

Lepore, S. J., Silver, R. C., Wortman, C. B., & Wayment, H. A. (1996). Social constraints, intrusive thoughts, and depressive symptoms among bereaved mothers. *Journal of Personality and Social Psychology, 70,* 271–282.

Neimeyer, R. A. (2006). Re-storying loss: Fostering growth in the posttraumatic narrative. In L. G. Calhoun & R. G. Tedeschi (Eds.), *Handbook of posttraumatic growth: Research and practice* (pp. 68–80). Mahwah, NJ: Lawrence Erlbaum Associates.

Neimeyer, R.A. (2010). Reconstructing the continuing bond: A constructivist approach to grief therapy. In J. D. Raskin, S. K. Bridges, & R. A. Neimeyer (Eds.), *Studies in meaning 4: Constructivist perspectives on theory, practice, and social justice* (pp. 65–91). New York, NY: Pace University Press.

Neimeyer, R. A., Burke, L. A., Mackay, M. M., & van Dyke Stringer, J. G. (2010). Grief therapy and the reconstruction of meaning: From principles to practice. *Journal of Contemporary Psychotherapy, 40(2)*, 73–83. doi:10.1007/s10879-009-9135-3

Nerken, I. R. (1993). Grief and the reflective self: Toward a clearer model of loss resolution and growth. *Death Studies, 17*, 1–26.

Oliver, L. E. (1999). Effects of a child's death on the marital relationship. *Omega: Journal of Death and Dying, 39*, 197–227.

Parkes, C. M. (1971). Psycho-social transitions: A field study. *Social Science and Medicine, 5*, 101–115.

Romanoff, B. D. (1993). When a child dies: Special considerations for providing mental health counseling for bereaved parents. *Journal of Mental Health Counseling, 15*, 384–393.

Rubin, S., & Malkinson, R. (2001). Parental response to child loss across the life cycle: Clinical and research perspectives. In M. S. Stroebe, R. O. Hansson, W. Stroebe, & H. Schut (Eds.), *Handbook of bereavement research: Consequences, coping, and care* (pp. 219–240). Washington, DC: American Psychological Association. doi:10.1037/10436-009

Staub, E., & Vollhardt, J. (2008). Altruism born of suffering: The roots of caring and helping after victimization and other trauma. *American Journal of Orthopsychiatry, 78*(3), 267–280. doi:10.1037/a0014223

Stroebe, M. S., & Schut, H. A. (1999). The dual process model of coping with bereavement: Rationale and description. *Death Studies, 23*, 197–224.

Taku, K., Cann, A., Calhoun, L. G., & Tedeschi, R. G. (2008). The factor structure of the Posttraumatic Growth Inventory: A comparison of five models using confirmatory factor analysis. *Journal of Traumatic Stress, 21*(2), 158–164. doi:10.1002/jts.20305

Taku, K., Tedeschi, R. G., Cann, A., & Calhoun, L. G. (2009). The culture of disclosure: Effects of perceived reactions to disclosure on posttraumatic growth and distress in Japan. *Journal of Social and Clinical Psychology, 28*(10), 1226–1243. doi:10.1521/jscp.2009.28.10.1226

Talbot, K. (1998-1999). Mothers now childless: Personal transformation after the death of an only child. *Omega: Journal of Death and Dying, 38*, 167–186.

Tedeschi, R. G., & Calhoun, L. G. (1995). *Trauma and transformation: Growing in the aftermath of suffering*. Thousand Oaks, CA: Sage Publications.

Tedeschi, R. G., & Calhoun, L. G. (1996). The Posttraumatic Growth Inventory: Measuring the positive legacy of trauma. *Journal of Traumatic Stress, 9,* 455–471.

Tedeschi, R. G., & Calhoun, L. G. (2004a). Posttraumatic growth: Conceptual foundations and empirical evidence. *Psychological Inquiry, 15,* 1–18.

Tedeschi, R. G., & Calhoun, L. G. (2004b). *Helping bereaved parents: A clinician's guide*. New York: Brunner-Routledge.

Tedeschi, R. G., & Calhoun, L. G. (2006). Expert companions: Posttraumatic growth in clinical practice. In L. G. Calhoun & R. G. Tedeschi (Eds.), *Handbook of posttraumatic growth: Research and practice* (pp. 291–310). Mahwah, NJ: Lawrence Erlbaum Associates.

Tedeschi, R. G., & Calhoun, L. G. (2010). A surprise attack, a surprise result: Posttraumatic growth through expert companionship. In G. W. Burns (Ed.), *Happiness, healing, enhancement: Your casebook collection for applying positive psychology in therapy* (pp. 226–236). Hoboken, NJ: John Wiley & Sons Inc.

van der Houwen, K., Stroebe, M., Schut, H., Stroebe, W., & van den Bout, J. (2010). Online mutual support in bereavement: An empirical examination. *Computers in Human Behavior, 26*(6), 1519–1525. doi:10.1016/j.chb.2010.05.019

Vicary, A. M., & Fraley, R. (2010). Student reactions to the shootings at Virginia Tech and Northern Illinois University: Does sharing grief and support over the Internet affect recovery? *Personality and Social Psychology Bulletin, 36*(11), 1555–1563. doi:10.1177/0146167210384880

Weiss, T., & Berger, R. (2010). Posttraumatic growth around the globe: Research findings and practice implications. In T. Weiss & R. Berger (Eds.) *Posttraumatic growth and culturally competent practice: Lessons learned from around the globe* (pp. 189–195). Hoboken, NJ: John Wiley & Sons Inc.

Wortman, C. B., & Silver, R. C. (1989). The myths of coping with loss. *Journal of Consulting and Clinical Psychology, 57,* 349–357.

Znoj, H. (2006). Bereavement and posttraumatic growth. In L. G. Calhoun & R.G. Tedeschi (Eds.), *Handbook of posttraumatic growth: Research and practice* (pp. 176–196). Mahwah, NJ: Lawrence Erlbaum Associates.

CHAPTER 6

Beyond Kübler-Ross: What We Have Learned About Grief From Cross-Cultural Research

Paul C. Rosenblatt

On Death and Dying (Kübler-Ross, 1969) was an amazingly influential book. It focused a powerful light on the neglected topics of dying, death, and bereavement. It insisted on the important linkage of spirituality to the issues psychologists, medical personnel, and social scientists dealt with, and provided a compelling account of how people deal with their own dying and death. The lessons in the book made it much easier to understand and deal compassionately with people who were dying. But half a century is a long time for ideas in any area to remain current and acceptable. Kübler-Ross's very success at stimulating research, writing, and practice innovations made it easier for work on dying, death, and bereavement to move beyond what she wrote.

Part of the success and acceptance of Kübler-Ross's thinking about the processes of dying and bereavement was that she wrote in a modernist way in modernist times. In this approach to writing and thinking, humans are generalized about as though we are all rather alike, and truths are offered with certainty. This modernist approach still exists in the study of dying and bereavement, but thanatologists and other researchers have become diverse, as have those they study. There are also influential postmodernist developments that see not truths and generalizations, but possibilities and a multiplicity of viewpoints. Kübler-Ross's view from 1969 might fit some people in some situations, but even in those instances, there could be other ways of understanding what is going on. And Kübler-Ross herself, in her posthumously published book on grief and grieving (Kübler-Ross & Kessler, 2005), made clear that she thought everyone's grief is unique, that generalizations, including the five stages, have their limitations.

The classic sources on bereavement—for example, Freud (1917) and Lindemann (1944)—were written and read as though culture was irrelevant. Research developed, practice studies were carried out, theoretical analyses were developed, a case study literature grew, and textbooks were written that offered a view of grieving in which culture did not matter. Earlier writings about grief, including the early work of Kübler-Ross, followed this pattern. The writings seemed to claim that there is a basic human pattern to grieving. No matter what a person's culture, we were all basically the same. Yet at the same time, a very substantial literature had developed, particularly in anthropology, that showed that culture does matter in trying to understand grief. Studies were conducted to explore the similarities, differences, and patterns in grief across cultures (e.g., Rosenblatt, Walsh, & Jackson, 1976). Now we have reached the point where every volume of the major thanatology journals includes articles exploring how culture shapes grieving. Many practitioners understand how important it is to attend to culture, and they work at being culturally knowledgeable with people they hope to help. Cross-cultural research offers a window into seeing where the field has gone since 1969 and to laying out both alternative modernist views of dying, death, and bereavement and also postmodern views. Cross-cultural studies of grief have taught us that if one wants to understand or help a grieving person, that person's cultural background matters enormously (Klass, 1999; Rosenblatt, 1993, 1997, 2001; Stroebe & Schut, 1998).

What have we learned from cross-cultural studies? Two major lessons have emerged. First, we have learned that knowledge and perspectives derived from one culture (including the social and psychological science of that culture) do not necessarily apply to other cultures. Second, we have learned basic ideas about how to become culturally sensitive helpers of grieving people.

Cultural Patterning of Grief

The cross-cultural literature has challenged us to back away from general statements about bereavement. Some aspects of how people grieve may be common across cultures, but it is a mistake to say that all humans grieve in a certain way. An even bigger mistake is to take the next step and assume that all grieving humans should behave in a certain way, or that there is something wrong with a bereaved person who does not react in a proscribed manner. Many aspects of grieving that once were assumed to be universal are now known to be characteristic of only some cultures—emotive expressions such as crying or visibly feeling sad or depressed; the processes of developing narratives about the death or the deceased; grieving over a defined time course, or experiencing grief in stages. Any generalization about grief misses the diversity of people across cultures and is probably wrong for billions of people. This fact forces a move away from claims like those of Kübler-Ross (1969) that all humans are the same to claims about what is possible or what fits specific people in specific cultures. In encountering someone who is grieving, our knowledge (of the literature and of practice) is a knowledge of possibility, not of certainty.

There is a cultural basis to what we have learned and think is true. In writings on grief from which we have learned, in our own language about grief, in our practice experience, powerful cultural forces are at work that shape and limit our sense of what grief is. We may think that we have learned about human nature, but we have learned one culture's way of classifying, framing, and making sense of things. These culturally-rooted views can have an aura of truth because we function in a community of people who think along the same lines, and perhaps because we do not know alternatives. Scholarly writings have a basis in research that gives them weight. However, seeing the thanatology one has learned as socioculturally constructed rather than truth that transcends culture encourages a critical, analytic perspective that can provide rich new insights (see, e.g., Walter, 2005–2006). Knowing that our own foundation for understanding grief is socially constructed opens us to the possibility that the realities of others—including the people we are trying to help—will be quite different (see, e.g., Lopez, 2006).

For example, in some cultures, for some deaths of close family members, people apparently grieve little or not at all (Scheper-Hughes, 1985, writing about child deaths among impoverished people in northeastern Brazil). In some cultures, people who have experienced major losses strive to appear upbeat and undistressed and are strongly supported in that effort by the people around them (Wikan, 1988). In other cultures, people try not to cry over a major loss, conceal feelings of distress, and try to get over the loss quickly (Whittaker, Hardy, Lewis, & Buchan, 2005, writing about Somalis). By contrast, it would be normal for an Egyptian woman who has experienced the death of a child to grieve through years of muted depression, withdrawal, inactivity, self-absorbtion, and palpable suffering (Wikan, 1988).

Nor is grief necessarily expressed through emotional channels, as is common in the United States. It may be somatized (Abu-Lughod, 1985, writing about Egyptian Bedouins; Fabrega & Nutini, 1994, writing about Mexican Tlaxcalans). If we do not understand a person's cultural code, we might not connect severe headaches or chest pain with grief. Grief is also expressed in some cultures through rage and violence, which is outside the experience of many people who work with the bereaved in North America, Europe, or East Asia (Robarchek & Robarchek, 2005, writing about the Waorani of Ecuador; Schiefflin, 1985, writing about the Kaluli of New Guinea).

In opening up to the realities of cultures that are outside our personal experience, we will learn that our language and concepts are not sufficient to understand core grief in some cultures. Some terms in the grief vocabulary of some cultures have no equivalent in English. For example, the Ifaluk, a Pacific island society, use the terms *lalomweiu* and *fago* (Lutz, 1985). *Lalomweiu* may be translated as a loneliness combined with sadness, as in "I *lalomweiu* my uncle who died." *Fago* may be translated as compassion combined with love and sadness; it is used primarily to talk about people one misses, as in "I *fago* my relatives who are away." The Ojibwe term *gashkendam* combines grief with loneliness, affliction, dejection, homesickness, and melancholy (McNally, 2000). Even language that seems to be very straightforward—for example, "I feel sad"—may have underlying cultural meanings and complexities that are outside of the experience of most English speakers. Thus, "I feel sad" may include feelings of fear, indignation, shame, or inadequacy.

There also is considerable diversity across cultures in what is grieved. We cannot assume that a person in another culture is weeping for the same reasons people in our own culture weep. For example, a widow might be weeping about the extreme poverty in which she now finds herself (Rosenblatt & Nkosi, 2007, writing about Zulu widows of South Africa). A Bumbita Arapesh man grieving the death of his father might be focused on his loss of mentorship and of help obtaining a wife (Leavitt, 1995). Part of a bereaved African American's sorrow about the death of a loved one might be related to the racism that limited what the loved one could do (educationally, occupationally, and in other ways) and made life more difficult for the loved one (Rosenblatt & Wallace, 2005). In Latin American societies in which military dictatorship and assassination squads have killed or "disappeared" many, grief over a death or disappearance may be entangled in feelings about the injustice of the violence, rage at those who instigated the violence, and fear that one could also be a victim (Hollander, 1997; Zur, 1998).

Some cultures have notions of what grieving should be like and what forms of grieving are not good, something like indigenous notions of grief pathology. For example, the Balinese worry about a grieving person who does not present a happy and smooth outer appearance (Wikan, 1990).

Mourning

Cultural practices in dealing with death and bereavement are key to the patterning of grief across cultures and inseparable from cultural diversity in the psychology of grieving. These practices may be focused on the deceased, the ancestors, efforts to determine the cause of death, protecting the bereaved, dealing with property, or protecting the community from spirits who might be dangerous. To understand a grieving person from another culture, we must understand the cultural requirements that shape what the person can or cannot do. For example, many cultures have a mourning period (often a year) during which bereaved people are limited in what they may do, where they may go, what they wear, their demeanor, and much more (Rosenblatt, Walsh, & Jackson, 1976). At the end of the mourning period, there is almost always a final ceremony that ends the mourning and deals with the spirit, and perhaps the remains, of the deceased. It may seem to an outsider that the grieving person is artificially limited and that her or his feelings, thoughts, and inclinations may be inconsistent with the requirements of ritual. But often, grieving people are comfortable with or adapt to whatever mourning rituals require of them.

During mourning periods, bereaved people may be isolated from most or all others and may be marked in special ways by what they wear or other changes in appearance (Rosenblatt, Walsh, & Jackson, 1976). These ritual practices give them time to grieve—in contrast, say, to the demands U.S. employers put on bereaved people to get back to work almost immediately after a significant death (Rosenblatt, 2000). Cultural practices may also organize and recruit help for a bereaved person, so the person is not alone in her or his grieving. For example, a bereaved person who is isolated from others may be helped by some in the community with drawing water and acquiring food. The help may seem to be material, but it may also be experienced as emotional support.

In many cultures, the mourning period includes relating to the spirit of the deceased. That spirit may be loved or feared; may be helped, supported, or appeased in various ways; or may be ignored. In some cultures, one must guard against harm from the spirit by, for example, never mentioning the deceased's name (Shepard, 2002, writing about the Matsigenka of Peru). The Jivaro, an Amazonian people, actively work at forgetting the deceased (Taylor, 1993), and the Haya of Tanzania work at forgetting some of the meanings attached to objects that had belonged to the deceased as a way of acknowledging that the deceased no longer had the connection he or she had to the objects and to the living (Weis, 1997). Often, the spirits of the deceased are considered more likely to be in contact with the living immediately after the death and possibly to be more troublesome than they will be later (Dernbach, 2005, writing about the Chuuk of Micronesia; Rosenblatt, Walsh, & Jackson, 1976, pp. 63–65).

The meanings of terms related to death and dying vary across cultures. Take, for example, the word "dead." In Oman, a person whose breathing has stopped is not necessarily considered dead (Al-Adawi, Burjorjee, & Al-Issa, 1997), even after considerable time of not breathing has passed. Among the Matsigenka of Peru (Shepard, 2002) some people are considered dead before they stop breathing, so those around them see no point to providing palliative medication. The cause of death is a sense-making matter in which cultures differ widely. The reasons Americans give for the death of a loved one and the causes that appear on U.S. death certificates are as much a reflection of our culture as, say, cultural accounts that focus on sorcery or witchcraft as a cause of death (e.g., Brison, 1992, writing about a cultural group in New Guinea; Mentore, 2005, writing about the Waiwai of Guyana; Rosenblatt & Nkosi, 2007, writing about the Zulu of South Africa).

Collective Grief

Much of the bereavement literature takes the individual as the unit of analysis. It is the individual who has the feelings and beliefs, and perhaps seeks help. But in many cultures, the death is considered a loss to the community, clan, or family, and grieving is collective. In these cultures, activities express the collective loss and deal with the problems the loss creates for the collective. To someone from an individually-focused culture, some of the grieving people may seem to be rather remotely related to the person whose loss they are grieving. Alternatively, one person might be, in a sense, the designated mourner (Francis, Kellaher, & Neophytou, 2005, p. 145)—the person among all those who are collectively grieving who carries the greatest responsibility for dealing in culturally appropriate and visible ways with the death.

The Culturally Sensitive Helper

The discussion so far in this chapter has shown how much more complex and diverse bereavement is across cultures than is implied by the simple analysis offered by Kübler-Ross (1969). Much of the scholarly and professional literature that assumes that humans are the same may often lead to a professional missing crucial aspects of grieving in the culture of a person one hopes to help. It is an easy mistake to make, and it is easy not even to recognize this as a mistake. In my early cross-cultural work on bereavement (Rosenblatt, Walsh, & Jackson, 1976), I was sure that our theories would fit people everywhere. I fit the available information from various cultures to the theories of that time, but in the process I dismissed or ignored information that did not fit those theories. I also interpreted information about grieving in cultures different from my own in ways that took me far from the true meanings, understandings, and experiences of people in those cultures.

I realize now that I was missing crucially important cultural realities. I have not come to distrust theory as a result, but I have become skeptical of "totalizing theory," theory that applies understanding, classification, and insight to all people everywhere. I have learned that cultural differences are enormous and very important. Trying to provide support to a widow from a culture different from my own, I cannot assume that widowhood—or death, grief, or support—means to her what they mean in my culture. I cannot assume that the stages Kübler-Ross wrote about are even remotely relevant to her grief process. Even the etiquette of my relationship with her may be far from what I know about etiquette in my own culture. Her responses to my questions and my offers of support may not mean what I think they mean. The very sources of her grief may not be what I assume; for example, she may be grieving the fact that, as a widow in an alien cultural setting, she has to deal with me! Even if I understand many things about her culture, I might not understand that she is resisting that culture. She might, for example, be trying to continue her grieving beyond the normal and accepted time in her culture and resisting angry pressure from others in her culture to conform to those standards (e.g., Maschio, 1992, writing about a widow on the Pacific island of New Britain). Even if she is doing the same things a widow in my own culture might do, the meaning may be very different—for example, a bereaved person in Taiwan (Hsu & Kahn, 1998-1999) may keep busy for very different reasons than one in the United States (Rosenblatt, 2000, pp. 56-57).

To complicate matters, the aspects of culture that deal with death and grief are not static. People can be quite creative in dealing with losses in ways that may change their culture for themselves and others (Oushankine, 2006, writing about Russian mothers who organized to deal with the deaths of soldier sons in ways that were new, though connected to preexisting aspects of their culture). Cultures are also changed through contact with other cultures (e.g., Lohmann, 2005, writing about the influence of Christian missionaries on a culture of Papua New Guinea). And cultures are not monolithic, clear in their demands and standards, or able to deal with every situation, so there may be quite a bit of diversity in how people in a culture mourn (Valentine, 2010, writing about the Japanese), or intense conflict may arise among people in a culture over matters relating to loss (e.g., Stewart & Strathern, 2005, writing about conflict over who has the right to bury a specific corpse in a Papua New Guinea cultural group).

Learning specifics about grief in various cultures can make us more humble, respectful, and competent in working with bereaved people from those cultures. This kind of knowledge can also illustrate the danger of a totalizing perspective. But it is easy to slide back to our own cultural beliefs and totalizing theories (Krause, 1998, p. 2), especially when the gap between us and a person from a different culture seems immense, but we think we should do something. Even with considerable cultural knowledge, we may not be able to help. But the more knowledge we have, the more open we are. We can do good with a knowledge of possibility rather than a certainty of truth.

In working with a community, a family, or an individual from a particular culture, we can read about grief in that culture and consult with cultural insiders who have relevant life experience and information or with outsiders who have studied the culture. We could, for example, acquire through reading or conversation a set of ideas about how the Hmong might deal with a death. However, we must treat that knowledge as something less than truth. No matter how much what we read and what the experts say, the people we work with might be different. Their subculture, their religious identity, or the cultural changes they have experienced may make our knowledge partially or completely irrelevant. Similarly, our understanding of what we have read or heard may involve simplifications or interpretations that render what we think we know inaccurate. Further, some people are not open about aspects of grief in their culture (e.g., Whittaker et al., 2005, writing about Somalis). So even the "expert sources" of information may be limited. Also, many people are bicultural or multicultural and thus blend grieving practices and traditions from more than one culture (Adams, 1993). It is necessary in working with people from any culture—even one we think we know—to learn from them what they can and are willing to teach us about what they want, believe, understand, feel, and struggle with.

One cost of cultural ignorance may be to see as pathology in a grieving person what is sane, normal, expected, meaningful, respected, and appropriate by the standards of that person's culture. Freud, in his influential 1917 essay

"Mourning and Melancholia", did not consider grieving, even in its extremes forms, to be pathological. But contemporary writers in the field have moved toward disciplining and narrowing the sense of what is acceptable grief by defining certain forms of grieving as pathology (Foote & Frank, 1999). Arguably some of what a grief expert sees as pathology in a person from another culture is seen that way because of the "knowledge" the expert brings from her or his own culture, but that knowledge can miss what is culturally normal in the grieving of a person from another culture. Ong (2003, pp. 106–108), for example, writes about Cambodian refugees in the United States who struggled to deal with a mental health clinic that was asking for words they were unwilling to say and offering them medications they feared would block their thoughts and feelings about their terrible losses in the "killings fields" of Cambodia. What seems pathological in one culture may be normal in another.

It might be most helpful to respect the grieving we witness rather than labeling it as pathological or not and to respond to it in ways appropriate to the culture of the person we wish to help. For example, we would allow the Zulu widow (Rosenblatt & Nkosi, 2007) to avoid eye contact with us, to sit behind us, and to claim to know nothing about the relevance of witchcraft to her situation (even though in her culture witchcraft is central). If a person needs help, perhaps that would be help with food, help with ceremonial expenses, and patient listening, rather than antidepressants, forced conversation, or trying to make that person's grief fit into our own cultural framework. And that is not so different from what Kübler-Ross did. Reading her 1969 book *On Death and Dying*, and her 2005, posthumously published book, *On Grief and Grieving*, she obviously was a sensitive listener, a person who was open to the diverse issues of different bereaved people, and above all a person who worked at learning from the dying and the bereaved, rather than a person who insensitively imposed her ways of thinking on them. These insights and modeled skills, rather than a model of stages, are the essential lessons we should draw from her groundbreaking work.

Editor's Note: This chapter was revised from Rosenblatt, P. C. (2007). Grief: What we have learned from cross-cultural studies. In K.J. Doka (Ed.), *Living with grief: Before and after the death*, Washington, DC: Hospice Foundation of America.

Paul C. Rosenblatt *has a PhD in psychology and is Morse-Alumni Distinguished Teaching Professor of Family Social Science at the University of Minnesota. He has authored or co-authored six books (including* African American Grief, *published in 2005 and co-authored by Beverly R. Wallace) and 54 scholarly articles and book chapters that focus on bereavement. Much of his other work touches on death, dying, and bereavement, including his recent book* Shared Obliviousness in Family Systems *(2009) and a current book project on how African-American novelists write about the impact of racism on African-American families. His current work also includes an essay on complicated grief from a cross-cultural perspective, an analysis (with Peter Rober) of family communication about a family death in James Agee's* A Death in the Family, *and an essay about complexities and ambiguities in defining "grief."*

References

Abu-Lughod, L. (1985). Honor and sentiments of loss in a Bedouin society. *American Ethnologist, 12,* 245–261.

Adams, K. M. (1993). The discourse of souls in Tana Toraja (Indonesia): Indigenous notions and Christian conceptions. *Ethnology, 32,* 55–68.

Al-Adawi, S., Burjorjee, R., & Al-Issa, I. (1997). Mu-ghayeb: A culture-specific response to bereavement in Oman. *International Journal of Social Psychiatry, 43,* 144–151.

Brison, K. J. (1992). *Just talk: Gossip, meetings, and power in a Papua New Guinea village.* Berkeley: University of California Press.

Dernbach, K. B. (2005). Spirits of the hereafter: Death, funerary possession, and the afterlife in Chuuk, Micronesia. *Ethnology, 44,* 99–123.

Fabrega, H., Jr., & Nutini, H. (1994). Tlaxcalan constructions of acute grief. *Culture, Medicine and Psychiatry, 18,* 405–431.

Foote, C. E., & Frank, A. W. (1999). Foucault and therapy: The disciplining of grief. In A. S. Chambon, A. Irving, & L. Epstein (Eds.), *Reading Foucault for social work* (pp. 157–187). New York: Columbia University Press.

Francis, D., Kellaher, L., & Neophytou, G. (2005). *The secret cemetery.* Oxford, England: Berg.

Freud, S. Mourning and melancholia. (1957). In J. Riviere (Ed.), *Collected papers of Sigmund Freud, vol. 4, Papers on metapsychology, Papers on applied psychoanalysis* (pp. 152–170). New York: Basic Books. (Originally published in 1917).

Hollander, N. C. (1997). *Love in a time of hate: Liberation psychology in Latin America.* New Brunswick, NJ: Rutgers University Press.

Hsu, M. T., & Kahn, D. L. (1998–1999). Coping strategies of Taiwanese widows adapting to loss. *Omega: Journal of Death and Dying, 38,* 269–288.

Klass, D. (1999). Developing a cross-cultural model of grief: The state of the field. *Omega: Journal of Death and Dying, 39,* 153–176.

Krause, I. B. (1998). *Therapy across culture.* Thousand Oaks, CA: Sage.

Kübler-Ross, E. (1969). *On death and dying.* New York: Macmillan.

Kübler-Ross, E., & Kessler, D. (2005). *On grief and grieving: Finding the meaning of grief through the five stages of loss.* New York: Scribner.

Leavitt, S. C. (1995). Seeking gifts from the dead: Long-term mourning in Bumbita Arapesh cargo narrative. *Ethos, 23,* 53–73.

Lindemann, E. (1944). Symptomatology and management of acute grief. *American Journal of Psychiatry, 101,* 141–148.

Lohmann, R. I. (2005). The afterlife as Asabano corpses: Relationships with the deceased in Papua New Guinea. *Ethnology, 44,* 189–206.

Lopez, S. A. (2006). The influence of culture and ethnicity on end-of-life care. In R. S. Katz & T. A. Johnson (Eds.), *When professionals weep: Emotional and countertransference responses in end-of-life care* (pp. 91–103). New York: Routledge.

Lutz, C. (1985). Depression and the translation of emotional worlds. In A. Kleinman & B. Good (Eds.), *Culture and depression* (pp. 63–100). Berkeley: University of California Press.

Maschio, T. (1992). To remember the faces of the dead: Mourning and the full sadness of memory in southwestern New Britain. *Ethos, 20,* 387–420.

McNally, M. D. (2000). *Ojibwe singers: Hymns, grief, and a native culture in motion.* New York: Oxford University Press.

Mentore, G. (2005). *Of passionate curves and desirable cadences: Themes on Waiwai social being.* Lincoln, NE: University of Nebraska Press.

Ong, A. (2003). *Buddha is hiding: Refugees, citizenship, the new America.* Berkeley: University of California Press.

Oushankine, S. A. (2006). The politics of pity: Domesticating loss in a Russian province. *American Anthropologist, 108,* 297–311.

Robarchek, C., & Robarchek, C. (2005). Waorani grief and the witch-killer's rage: Worldview, emotion, and anthropological explanation. *Ethos, 33,* 205–230.

Rosenblatt, P. C. (1993). Cross-cultural variation in the experience, expression, and understanding of grief. In D. P. Irish, K. F. Lundy, & V. J. Nelsen (Eds.), *Ethnic variations in dying, death, and grief: Diversity in universality* (pp. 13–19). Washington, DC: Taylor & Francis.

Rosenblatt, P. C. (1997). Grief in small scale societies. In C. M. Parkes, P. Laungani, & B. Young (Eds.), *Death and bereavement across cultures* (pp. 27–51). London: Routledge.

Rosenblatt, P. C. (2000). *Help your marriage survive the death of a child.* Philadelphia: Temple University Press.

Rosenblatt, P. C. (2001). A social constructionist perspective on cultural differences in grief. In M. S. Stroebe, R. O. Hansson, W. Stroebe, & H. Schut (Eds.), *Handbook of bereavement research: Consequences, coping, and care* (pp. 285–300). Washington, DC: American Psychological Association.

Rosenblatt, P. C., & Nkosi, B. C. (2007). South African Zulu widows in a time of poverty and social change. *Death Studies, 31,* 67–85.

Rosenblatt, P. C., & Wallace, B. R. (2005). Narratives of grieving African-Americans about racism in the lives of deceased family members. *Death Studies, 29,* 217–235.

Rosenblatt, P. C., Walsh, R. P., & Jackson, D. A. (1976). *Grief and mourning in cross cultural perspective.* New Haven, CT: Human Relations Area Files Press.

Scheper-Hughes, N. (1985). Culture, scarcity and maternal thinking: Maternal detachment and infant survival in a Brazilian shantytown. *Ethos, 13,* 291–317.

Schiefflin, E. L. (1985). The cultural analysis of depressive affect: An example from New Guinea. In A. Kleinman & B. J. Good (Eds.), *Culture and depression* (pp. 101–133). Berkeley: University of California Press.

Shepard, G. H., Jr. (2002). Three days for weeping: Dreams, emotions, and death in the Peruvian Amazon. *Medical Anthropology Quarterly, 16,* 200–229.

Stewart, P. J., & Strathern, A. (2005). Cosmology, resources, and landscape: Agencies of the dead and the living in Duna, Papua New Guinea. *Ethnology, 44,* 35–47.

Stroebe, M., & Schut, H. (1998). Culture and grief. *Bereavement Care, 17*(1), 7–11.

Taylor, A. C. (1993). Remembering to forget: Identity, mourning and memory among the Jivaro. *Man, 28,* 653–678.

Valentine, C. (2010). The role of the ancestral tradition in bereavement in contemporary Japanese society. *Mortality, 15,* 275–293.

Walter, T. (2005–2006). What is complicated grief? A social constructionist perspective. *Omega: Journal of Death and Dying, 52,* 71–79.

Weis, B. (1997). Forgetting your dead: Alienable and inalienable objects in northwest Tanzania. *Anthropological Quarterly, 70,* 164–172.

Whittaker, S., Hardy, G., Lewis, K., & Buchan, L. (2005). An exploration of psychological well-being with young Somali refugee and asylum-seeker women. *Clinical Child Psychology and Psychiatry, 10,* 177–196.

Wikan, U. (1988). Bereavement and loss in two Muslim communities: Egypt and Bali compared. *Social Science and Medicine, 27,* 451–460.

Wikan, U. (1990). *Managing turbulent hearts: A Balinese formula for living.* Chicago: University of Chicago Press.

Zur, J. N. (1998). *Violent memories: Mayan war widows in Guatemala.* Boulder, CO: Westview.

PART III

Implications for Practice

The final three chapters explore some of the current debates that will likely continue to shape our understandings of grief. Colin Murray Parkes begins this section by discussing the ways that the newest *Diagnostic and Statistical Manual of Mental Disorders (DSM-5)* will address current research and understandings of grief. In many ways, this reflects the question that Freud (1917) posed in "Mourning and Melancholia": When is grief simply a normal response to loss and at what point does it become more problematic? At present a number of alternatives are being considered—that Acute Grief rather than Bereavement should be a "V-Code" (other conditions that may be a focus of clinical attention); that the Bereavement Exclusion be removed from the diagnosis of a Major Depressive Episode; and that a new category, "Adjustment Disorder Related to Bereavement," be included. Parkes makes a forceful argument in favor of the inclusion of Prolonged Grief Disorder as *one* form of complicated grief, leaving the door open to the future identification of other forms of complicated grief.

Louis Gamino adds a chapter about another current debate within the field— the effectiveness of grief counseling. In reviewing the history and research underlying this debate, Gamino echoes a point made in the discussions of the inclusion of grief-related conditions in *DSM-5*. Clearly many grievers are resilient. Only a small percentage of grieving individuals have more complicated reactions that merit professional intervention. Gamino makes another significant point. When grieving individuals are carefully screened and troubled grievers are assisted with empirically validated methods by counselors trained in the most current approaches, grief counseling can and does help.

Robert Neimeyer closes this section by examining current approaches toward treatment. Using a theatrical metaphor, Neimeyer proposes rather than utilizing stages, grief counselors should consider themselves as "stage managers" helping individuals to reconstruct and redirect their lives after a loss. Neimeyer offers an intriguing suggestion as to the continued popularity of stage theories even in the face of logical inconsistencies and the lack of empirical support. Stage theories retain popularity since they follow the structure of the myth of a heroic quest in which the protagonist suffers adversity but emerges transformed by the event. Neimeyer's chapter shows an impressive array of clinical tools that the counselor can employ to assist clients in reconstructing their own individual narratives now disrupted by loss. The individuality inherent in such an approach demonstrates forcefully the array of clinical possibilities once we move beyond Kübler-Ross.

CHAPTER 7

Complicated Grief in the *DSM-5*: Problems and Solutions

Colin Murray Parkes

Abstract

Although there is much evidence that grief sometimes takes a form that merits inclusion in the *Diagnostic and Statistical Manual of Mental Disorders (DSM)* of the American Psychiatric Association (APA), a major categorical error has resulted in its designation as Complicated Grief Disorder and, more recently, Bereavement Related Disorder. Here it is argued that both of these terms are misleading, implying, as they do, that only one such disorder exists. As a result, clinical psychiatrists have been forced to ignore the algorithm that has emerged from well-conducted research in order to include more than one clinical entity within a single diagnostic rubric. The result is imprecise, illogical, and confusing.

It is argued here that current data support Prigerson, Vanderwerker and Maciejewski's (2008) designation of this disorder as Prolonged Grief Disorder (PGD) thereby leaving open the possibility that other forms of complicated grief may subsequently be identified. In order to resolve the misunderstandings that have arisen, the nomenclature of grief and loss is here reviewed and a psychopathology that accords well with the risk factors for PGD is proposed. This identifies PGD as a disorder of attachment, akin to the Separation Anxiety Disorder of Childhood, and explains how that disorder gives rise to increased sensitivity to traumatic losses and difficulties in adjustment to bereavement. It also explains the success of recent treatment programs that have passed the test of random allocation.

During the last decade there has been a great increase in research into the psychological problems that can follow bereavement. The number of theoretical, empirical, and clinical studies reflects a bewildering variety of points of view. These have been well reviewed by Prigerson, Vanderwerker, and Maciejewski (2008), Boelen and Prigerson (in preparation), and by several other authors. Consequently this author has no need to give detailed justification for those conclusions that are now generally agreed upon.

In this paper we identify the major issues on which experts are in agreement and discuss some areas in which they appear to disagree. Given the number of authorities, the result seems to be a remarkably consistent overall picture, which gives us the basis for 1) a justifiable place for at least one complication of grief in the *DSM-5*; 2) a theoretical model that makes sense of the empirical data; and 3) indications that the condition can be treated with a reasonable chance of success. Differences arise in the terms used to designate the syndrome, some of the criteria for diagnosis, and its place in the diagnostic system of the *DSM*.

Problems of Nomenclature

Many of the differences that have arisen between bereavement researchers boil down to imprecise use of language. Perhaps the commonest mistakes have been to confuse *bereavement, grief,* and *mourning*.

Leading authorities today have reached a consensus that *bereavement* is the experience of loss of a loved person (or other object of attachment). Because bereavement can have many consequences the term simply defines a population but tells us little about the response.

Grief includes those emotional and cognitive reactions that are peculiar to the loss of an object of attachment. This means that it includes only those emotions and reactions that are distinct from the many nonspecific consequences of bereavement that can also occur following other types of stress. For instance, grief does not include depression, anxiety, or post-traumatic stress disorder, any and all of which can occur for a variety of reasons in addition to bereavement. The emotion that is the *sine qua non* of grief is *pining or yearning for the lost person* who is intensely missed. It is subjectively identical with the emotion of *separation anxiety* (more correctly, *separation distress*) that is the term used for the emotional response to threatened or actual separations from loved persons, even those that are temporary.

Considerable confusion has resulted from two different meanings given to the term *mourning*. In common parlance mourning is the public reaction to loss as witnessed by others. Thus many people may feel grief but "put on a brave face" at the funeral; others may put on a public display of mourning that has little to do with their felt emotion. This usage is favored by sociologists and most serious researchers, except psychoanalysts for whom, following Freud, mourning is a job of work defined as "a set of mental processes, conscious and unconscious, initiated by the loss of an emotionally and instinctually cathected object" (*International Dictionary of Psychoanalysis*). Many psychoanalysts use the terms grief and mourning interchangeably.

Given this ambiguity it is not surprising that confusion has arisen with regard to the terms with which atypical or abnormal forms of grieving are described. In recent years the earlier terms "morbid grief," "pathologic(al) grief," and "traumatic grief" have given place to Complicated Grief and, in the proposed fifth edition of the *DSM (DSM-5)*, Bereavement Related Disorder. Much discussion has taken place regarding the criteria for diagnosis of this condition on the assumption that it is a unitary phenomenon, i.e., that there is only one form of complicated grief or one major category with possible subcategories. This has led to attempts by various authors to include a wide range of features, many of which belong in different forms of complicated grief, and others that reflect the many nonspecific psychiatric complications (notably Clinical Anxiety, Major Depression, and Post-Traumatic Stress Disorder) that can be triggered by bereavement.

Prigerson's group has used sophisticated statistical methods to clarify these issues. Their Inventory of Complicated Grief (ICG), first developed in 1995, has provided us with a useful tool to measure those features of problematic bereavement that co-vary and can be clearly distinguished from both normal grief and the nonspecific complications of bereavement (Prigerson, Maciejewski, Newsom, Reynolds, Frank et al., 1995). While their questionnaire is not intended to replace clinical judgment, it has been found to correlate sufficiently well with clinical assessments to justify its use as a research tool. It has also enabled clinicians to refine their diagnostic criteria. What has emerged is a distinct syndrome, characterized by the persistence of disabling and distressing grief, along with other symptoms, that together deserve recognition as a distinct psychiatric disorder.

This said, there can be little doubt that future research will identify other forms of complicated grief. In the Harvard Bereavement Study of young Boston widows and widowers, Parkes and Weiss (1983) distinguished Chronic Grief from Conflicted Grief, two conditions with very different symptomatology and psychopathology; others will be described below. To avoid possible ambiguities, Prigerson, Vanderwerker, and Maciejewski (2008) have proposed the term Prolonged Grief Disorder (PGD) as a title for the syndrome and it is this that deserves consideration for inclusion in *DSM-5* (Prigerson, Horowitz, Jacobs, Parkes, Aslan et al., 2009). Objections to the title have been made on the grounds that this syndrome is very much more than a simple prolongation of normal grief. Psychiatrists today are sensitive to the charge that they are medicalizing normal life crises. Prigerson and her colleagues have gone to great lengths to demonstrate a cluster of associated symptoms that distinguish this syndrome (p. *v.i.*) and, together, bring about "clinically significant impairment in social, occupational, or other important areas of functioning (e.g., domestic responsibilities)."

Another group, headed by Katherine Shear, which uses the term Complicated Grief Disorder, is now in contention with Prigerson's group on the grounds that some of those whom they believe to be suffering complicated grief do not report "intense yearning for the deceased" (Shear, Simon, Wall, Zisook, Neimeyer et al., 2011). The members of Shear's group wish to include in their diagnosis those who "experience intrusive thoughts or preoccupation with the deceased." Yet yearning, pining, or intensely missing a lost person is the defining criterion of grief. Intrusive thoughts and preoccupation with the deceased, *in the absence of yearning*, sound more like obsessional reactions to bereavement and resemble the intrusive thoughts typical of Post-Traumatic Stress Disorder (PTSD) rather than Prolonged Grief Disorder. They may also reflect conflicted grief. If they are indeed a form of complicated grief they require a separate diagnostic appellation; in other words, Prigerson's syndrome is probably a separate disorder from this component of Shear's syndrome. Other complications that would not give rise to high scores on the ICG, yet are both complications of grieving and deserve further research, include identification syndromes in which bereaved people develop hypochondriacal illnesses resembling the illness from which a loved person has died, and compulsive blaming in which survivors postpone their grief to right a supposed injustice that they blame for the death or suffering of the loved person. While this is sometimes a logical and appropriate thing to do, it is commonly the case that the injustice is either unjustifiable or quite out of proportion to the true situation. Compulsive blaming is a common cause of complaints against medical services (Parkes & Prigerson, 2009).

Clearly much more research is needed in order to distinguish these various disorders. There is no way in which all of these bereavement-related disorders could be identified by means of a single algorithm. At this time, only one such disorder has been shown to meet the rigorous criteria expected by the authors of the *DSM*, Prigerson's PGD. Since this is the most common complication of bereavement it is likely to co-exist with other complications, thereby adding to the likelihood of confusion.

The Arguments for and Against Regarding Prolonged Grief Disorder as a Mental Illness

Most experts agree that there are times when grief persists for great lengths of time and is associated with much suffering and interference with the health and functions that make life worthwhile (see, for instance, a Special Edition of *Omega* edited by Parkes in 2006). Bereaved people commonly seek help for this problem and Prigerson's group calculate that, in the United States, about 10% of deaths from nontraumatic causes give rise to a case of PGD; traumatic deaths increase the risk. They estimate that one million Americans each year will suffer PGD. Much research indicates that they are at special risk of suicide, that their physical health is likely to be impaired, and that the condition increases the risk of a variety of psychiatric illnesses (reviewed in Prigerson et al., 2009). On the face of it they would seem to meet all of the criteria for a psychiatric disorder.

Opponents argue that: 1) prolonged grief disorder is not an illness but a normal reaction to an abnormal situation; 2) it is unfair to stigmatize bereaved people with the added burden of a psychiatric diagnosis; 3) such a diagnosis undermines self-esteem and encourages dependency on doctors and medication in people who need to become autonomous; 4) non-psychiatrists can be trained to provide the help that is needed; and 5) the whole enterprise is a form of medical imperialism.

These arguments can, of course, be applied to most psychiatric disorders, short of psychosis. They reflect commonly-held misunderstandings, distrust, and prejudices against psychiatry and psychiatrists. One of the misunderstandings is a failure to recognize that many psychiatric conditions are comprehensible reactions to abnormal situations (it is one of the aims of psychotherapies to unravel the chains of causation). Far from a psychiatric diagnosis being an added burden, PGD sufferers have been found to welcome the knowledge that they have a recognized and treatable condition, that they are not going mad (i.e., psychotic), and that their grief is not a self-indulgence or weakness (Prigerson & Maciejewski, 2006). Most doctors are all too aware of the dangers of encouraging dependency, more so than most of the other helpers to whom people with PGD will turn. In addition, doctors with proper training are aware of the research that shows that people with PGD do not benefit from antidepressants or other drugs and favor psychological treatments whose ultimate aim is to facilitate autonomy. In this situation, charges of medical imperialism are both prejudicial and unfair. Doctors deserve respect for their rigorous training, their respect for evidence-based knowledge of medicine, and their observation of a high standard of clinical practice. In a nationwide study of a Norwegian population of parents who had lost a child, 74% of whom met Prigerson's criteria for complicated grief, Dyregrov concluded, "by claiming to protect the individual from being powerless and dependent on professionals, the demedicalization strategy prevents people in psychosocial crisis [from obtaining] access to professional help" (2005, p. 9).

It is true that, at the present time, most doctors (including psychiatrists) are not a reliable source of help to bereaved people. As long as they do not see any form of grief as an illness, it is not their business to give help; they either dismiss the PGD sufferer or confuse complicated grief with major depression, anxiety disorders, or PTSD. On the other hand, there are some organizations, such as Cruse Bereavement Care in the United Kingdom, who are selecting, training, and supporting volunteers to provide a high quality of front-line help to the bereaved. This is a cost-effective response to many of the problems of bereavement and has been shown to reduce the need for medical care (Relf, 1998). However, it is a tall order to expect volunteers to provide the sophisticated therapies for PGD that have passed the test of random allocation studies (p. *vi*).

The inclusion of PGD in the *DSM-5* would make it a requirement of medical educators to teach doctors to diagnose the condition and for healthcare providers to ensure that appropriate treatment is available from properly trained experts. It would also stimulate research into the further refinement of the diagnosis and treatment of the complications of bereavement. Patients would become entitled to treatment under existing healthcare systems, and those whose bereavement was occasioned by human error or deliberate acts would become entitled to compensation.

Clearly the arguments for regarding PGD as a mental disorder are compelling; but PGD is only one of several conditions that can complicate grief. More research is needed to develop the criteria for diagnosis of these other conditions as Prigerson and others have done for PGD. In the meantime it has been a major error to attempt to lump them all together under the generic titles of Complicated Grief or Bereavement Related Disorder.

CRITERIA FOR PROLONGED GRIEF DISORDER

It would take us beyond the scope of this chapter to trace the long process of experimental testing of clinical hypotheses that have brought us from Lindemann's early work (1944) to the finely-tuned multivariate studies that have enabled Holly Prigerson to earn a place as one of the foremost researchers in the field of complicated disorders of grieving. It is her scrupulous attention to the evidence that has attracted an impressive group of clinicians to work with her to refine the diagnosis of the most common of these complications, Prolonged Grief Disorder.

Criteria for Prolonged Grief Disorder (as proposed to the *DSM-5* Trauma, PTSD, Dissociative and Anxiety Work Group by Prigerson, H.G., Horowitz, M.J. and Maciejewski, P.K. on March 3, 2010).

Separation Distress: to a daily or distressing or disruptive degree:
1. Yearning, pining, longing for the lost person
2. Intense feelings of emotional pain, sorrow, or pangs of grief

Cognitive, Emotional, Behavioral Symptoms: 5+ to a daily or distressing or disruptive degree:
1. Confusion about one's identity (e.g., one's role in life or diminished sense of self; feeling that a part of oneself has died)
2. Difficulty accepting the loss
3. Avoidance of reminders of the reality of the loss
4. Inability to trust others since the loss
5. Bitterness or anger related to the loss
6. Difficulty moving on with life (e.g., making new friends, pursuing interests); feeling stuck in grief
7. Numbness (absence of emotion) since the loss
8. Feeling that life is unfulfilling, empty, and meaningless since the loss
9. Feeling stunned, dazed, or shocked by the loss

Duration: Duration at least six months from the onset of separation distress.

Impairment: The above symptomatic disturbance causes clinically significant distress or impairment in social, occupational, or other important areas of functioning (e.g., domestic responsibilities).

These authors reported that people meeting these criteria can be reliably diagnosed with only 6% of positive and no negative errors. They can be clearly distinguished from those experiencing normal grief and from bereaved people suffering Major Depression or Generalized Anxiety Disorder (although these conditions often co-exist). These findings have been replicated and confirmed in people suffering different losses, and having various relationships to deceased, different circumstances of the loss, various times from the death, and living in ten culturally diverse countries. They showed that PGD is associated with a rise in hospital admissions and accidents, an increased risk of suicidal ideation, increased risk of life-threatening health events (myocardial infarction, cancer, and stroke), high blood pressure, and sleep disturbance through the first year of bereavement and with most of the health effects persisting for at least another year (Prigerson et al., 1997).

THE PSYCHOPATHOLOGY OF PROLONGED GRIEF DISORDER

Although the symptomatology of this condition has been developed out of clinical hunches and empirical observations, the syndrome is associated with a remarkably consistent pattern of predisposing factors which, taken together, give rise to a reasonable explanation for the causes of PGD and provide a logical basis for the treatments that are already proving successful.

As long ago as 1983 Parkes and Weiss demonstrated that 84% of young widows and widowers who reacted to the death of their spouse with severe and lasting yearning were rated as having been "highly dependent," whereas this was the case in only 16% of those with less yearning. We wrote, "Our data seem to us to provide support for Bowlby's notion that emotional dependence is a form of insecure attachment and that the tendency to form insecure attachments is usually determined in childhood" (Parkes & Weiss, 1983, p. 135). Subsequent systematic studies by Parkes, of older people seeking psychiatric help after bereavement, provided ample confirmation of our guess that there was a significant correlation between retrospective scores of anxious-ambivalent (clinging) attachments to parents in childhood and both clinging in adult life and persistently high scores of grief/loneliness after bereavement (Parkes, 2006b, pp. 77–88). Indeed, there were indications that high scores of anxious-ambivalent attachment in childhood had often amounted to what would today be classified as Separation Anxiety Disorder of Childhood; Parkes's data showed that this often lasts into adult life and is associated with persistent grief after bereavement (pp. 227–235). A similar study by Vanderwerker, Jacobs, Parkes, & Prigerson (2006) showed that a score based on recollections of high separation anxiety in childhood correlated significantly with PGD as measured by Prigerson's ICG (Prigerson et al., 1995).

The human brain contains a rich store of assumptions about the world, some of which are mutually contradictory. This is most obvious after bereavement when it is perfectly normal to treat a dead person as if he or she were still, to some degree, alive, and when it takes time for those most attached to the dead person to accept the full reality of their loss and its implications; "I can't believe it's true" is a common response. The primary function of crying after separation is to get back the lost person and it is perfectly normal for newly bereaved people to search for some way back to the lost person, visiting places and treasuring objects associated with them. Only as time passes do we accept the full reality of the loss and stop crying. In terms of learning theory, the cry becomes extinguished by nonreinforcement; but learning theory also teaches us that behavior that has been learned in conditions of intermittent reinforcement—e.g., when a mother is inconsistent in her response to her baby's cry—is particularly resistant to extinction. The child learns that it must cry and search hard and long if it is to get a response. In common with other attachment behavior learned in early childhood this assumption is likely to persist. It seems likely that this may explain the urge to cry and to search in bereaved people who experienced insecure attachments in childhood.

A fascinating finding of research into brain activity by means of fMRI scanning is the discovery that, compared with other bereaved people, those with PGD are more likely to respond to pictures of the lost person with immediate stimulation of the nucleus accumbens (Gundel et al., 2003; O'Connor et al., 2008). The nucleus accumbens is commonly known as the "pleasure center" of the brain and plays a central part in the reward circuits. If, as we suppose, the sufferer from PGD is engaging in a persistent search for a lost person, it is understandable that exposure to an image of that person will evoke an immediate reaction of reward. But this is only very transitory, for the nucleus accumbens is linked to other areas of the brain and the rewarding stimulus is soon disallowed. Consequently the overall emotional effect is disappointment rather than gratification. Similar results have been obtained with cocaine addicts who are shown triggers such as syringes (Maas, Scott, Lukas, Kaufman, Weis et al., 1998). The similarity between the pining of a PGD sufferer, who is missing a person, and the craving of the drug addict, who is missing a drug, is compelling.

These observations provide us with a probable explanation for persistent grief, but what of the other symptoms of PGD? These seem to reflect difficulties in adjusting to life in the absence of the loved person and they reflect the ways in which our security and sense of purpose and meaning are tied up with the security of our attachments. The evidence-base of the following section is described and referenced in detail in Parkes, 2006b. Bowlby pointed out that the function of attachment is to provide security. In the environment in which we evolved, many children were lost to predators and other dangers; it was important for survival that children stayed close to their parents and their home, and that parents responded rapidly to cries of distress. At the same time it was equally important that the children eventually learn to become autonomous rather than clinging to their parents. The children of secure attachments, whose parents respond consistently to potential dangers, providing protection when it is needed and reassurance when it is not, become more confident in themselves, more relaxed, and more trusting of others than those with insecure attachments. Conversely the children of insecure attachments grow up more insecure, less autonomous, and less able to deal confidently with trauma and major changes in life, particularly bereavements. As Prigerson et al. have shown (2010), their problems include difficulty in accepting the full reality of the loss and difficulty in moving forward without the person on whom they had previously relied. Their experiences in childhood have left them with negative expectations and pessimistic assumptions about their ability to survive without the lost person. These are most evident when the bereavement was unexpected and/or untimely. Having had no opportunity to prepare in advance for the loss, they are abruptly thrown into a dangerous world for which they feel unprepared.

These two components of grief—the urge to search for the lost person and the urge to move on in life without them—have been termed, by Stroebe and Schut (1999), the *loss orientation* and the *restoration orientation*. Both are necessary if people are to come through the dual process of grieving but, as they cannot take place simultaneously, bereaved people oscillate between them with the loss orientation predominating during the pangs of grief and the restoration orientation predominating during attempts to revise assumptions and internal models of the world.

In normal grief the loss orientation is most powerful and protracted during the early stages of grief but diminishes over time as the search for the lost person "out there" is extinguished. It then becomes possible for the bereaved to realize that there is a very real sense in which the dead person was never lost "in here." When bereaved people say, "He (or she) lives on in my memory," this is literally true. Many of the plans, habits of thought, and behavior that involved the other person during their lifetime continue to influence bereaved people and may even enrich their lives after bereavement. Hence, grieving is a gradual process of teasing out those thoughts and behaviors that are now obsolete, including the need to search, and replacing them with thoughts and behavior that remain meaningful in the next phase of life.

PGD complicates both processes. The loss orientation continues to dominate the mind, and difficulty in letting go of the person "out there" and accepting the loss interferes with the revision of the internal model of the world that facilitates a *continuing bond* (see Klass, Silverman & Nickman, 1996, for further discussion of continuing bonds).

CLINICAL IMPLICATIONS

Although there is little evidence that traditional methods of counseling are beneficial when provided to unselected samples of bereaved people, good results have been obtained for special services to the minority for whom the support of family and friends is not adequate to their needs (Kato & Mann, 1999). This includes all those who meet criteria for PGD. The services need to be tailored to the particular problems they bring. For instance, nortriptyline medication may help those who are clinically depressed but systematic research has shown that it is of no benefit to those who suffer from PGD (Reynolds et al., 1999).

At the time of writing two therapies have passed the test of random allocation and others are in the pipeline. The first of these was developed by Shear et al. (2005) for the treatment of her version of Complicated Grief (p. *vs*), in which most would have met criteria for PGD despite the differences indicated above. It comprises a battery of interventions in which, in the course of 16 weekly sessions, the client is helped, successively, to understand the dual process, to identify positive and negative memories by means of 'revisiting exercises,' to identify goals, and to monitor progress. Ninety-five bereaved patients were assigned at random to either this Complicated Grief Treatment (CGT) or to 16 weekly sessions of Interpersonal Psychotherapy. Differences between the groups began to emerge at 12 weeks and by 24 weeks there were significant differences in measures favoring the CGT group using Prigerson's ICG, the Beck Depression Inventory, and a measure of Work and Social Adjustment.

A similar intervention, using the techniques of Cognitive Behavior Therapy (CBT) was developed by Boelen, de Keijser, van den Hout, and van den Bout (2007). They assigned 54 bereaved people with high scores on Prigerson's ICG (25+), at random, to 12 weekly sessions of CBT or supportive psychotherapy. The CBT involved six sessions of exposure therapy, in which they were instructed to write down memories and thoughts about the lost person along with places and people that they tend to avoid, and six sessions of cognitive restructuring in which negative assumptions were identified and challenged. At the conclusion of treatment and 12 months later, significantly greater reduction in ICG scores was found in those who received CBT rather than supportive psychotherapy.

Boelen's exposure therapy and Shear's revisiting exercise sound very similar and Boelen's cognitive restructuring may well have been included in Shear's restoration orientation, which includes identifying goals. Both can be seen as consistent with the psychopathology described above. Thus, systematic and repeated exposure to memories of the loss and the lost person is a reasonable approach to the extinction of behavior patterns (searching for a lost person) that have resisted extinction by nonreinforcement. A similar form of guided mourning was used by Gauthier and Marshall (1977) and by Ramsey (1979), but without cognitive restructuring. It was evaluated (by Mawson et al., 1981) in a random allocation study. At the end of treatment and on follow-up 10 to 28 weeks later, the guided mourning group were able to talk and think more easily about their loss than those who had been instructed to avoid it, but their mental health was only slightly better than that of the comparison group.

Repeated exposure may overcome persistent seeking but it does nothing for the second component in the dual process, restoration. The addition of cognitive restructuring to the therapy is a logical way of helping the PGD sufferer to get back on course, but it is unlikely to succeed as long as the search for the lost person dominates thinking. When Boelen offered cognitive restructuring *before* exposure, benefits were less evident.

DSM-5: CURRENT CONSIDERATIONS

DSM-5 is expected to appear in May 2013. The committee has drafted changes to *DSM-IV-TR* and published them on the web for comment; these include important changes to the diagnosis of the psychiatric consequences of bereavement. Chief among these is the inclusion, within the section headed "G06 Adjustment Disorders," of a heading "Related to Bereavement." This reads:

> For at least 12 months following the death of a close relative or friend, the individual experiences, on more days than not, intense yearning/longing for the deceased, intense sorrow and emotional pain, or preoccupation with the deceased or the circumstances of the death. The person may also display difficulty accepting the death, intense anger over the loss, a

diminished sense of self, a feeling that life is empty, or difficulty planning for the future or engaging in activities or relationships. Mourning shows substantial cultural variation; the bereavement reaction must be out of proportion or inconsistent with cultural or religious norms.

This recognition that complicated forms of grief need to be distinguished from other psychiatric diagnoses is a major step forward, but the form of words chosen is a hodgepodge of generalizations that lacks the clinical precision that readers have come to expect of previous editions of this influential organ.

To do the committee justice, they have also made an attempt, in an appendix, to include a list of criteria for "Bereavement Related Disorder," designated as *for further study*.

BEREAVEMENT RELATED DISORDER *(Italics show differences from PGD)*.

A. The person experienced the *death* of a close relative or friend at least *12 months* earlier.

B. Since the death at least one of the following symptoms is experienced on more days than not and to a clinically significant degree:
1. Persistent yearning/longing for the deceased
2. Intense sorrow and emotional pain because of the death
3. *Preoccupation with the deceased person*
4. *Preoccupation with the circumstances of the death*

C. Since the death, *at least 6* of the following symptoms are experienced on more days than not and to a clinically significant degree:
Reactive Distress to the Death
1. Marked difficulty accepting the death
2. Feeling shocked, stunned, or emotionally numb over the loss
3. *Difficulty in positive reminiscing about the deceased*
4. Bitterness or anger related to the loss
5. *Maladaptive appraisals about oneself in relation to the deceased or the death (e.g., self-blame)*
6. Excessive avoidance of reminders of the loss *(e.g., avoiding places or people associated with the deceased)*

(continued on page 106)

> *Social/Identity Disruption*
> 7. *A desire not to live in order to be with the deceased*
> 8. Difficulty trusting other people since the death
> 9. *Feeling alone or detached from other people since the death*
> 10. Feeling that life is meaningless or empty without the deceased, or the belief that one cannot function without the deceased
> 11. Confusion about one's role in life or a diminished sense of one's identity (e.g., feeling that a part of oneself died with the deceased)
> 12. Difficulty or reluctance to pursue interests since the loss or to plan for the future (e.g., friendships, activities)
>
> D. The disturbance causes clinically significant distress or impairment in social, occupational, or other important areas of functioning
> E. *Mourning shows substantial cultural variation; the bereavement reaction must be out of proportion or inconsistent with cultural or religious norms*

This includes most of Prigerson's criteria but the committee has fallen into the trap of attempting to characterize all bereavement related disorders within a single algorithm. They claim that only one of the following is seen as necessary to the diagnosis: 1. Persistent yearning/longing for the deceased; 2. Intense sorrow and emotional pain because of the death; 3. Preoccupation with the deceased person; or 4. Preoccupation with the circumstances of the death. This means, for instance, that the preoccupation that results from long-standing ambivalence to the dead person, or the rage that results from a death by murder or manslaughter, is assumed to give rise to the same pattern of response as lifelong dependency, a claim that is not confirmed by clinical experience. Prigerson makes no such claim and includes only the first two criteria, both of which must be present and both of which constitute a severe form of grief. Other differences (shown in italics) are less crucial.

How Should PGD Be Categorized?

Horowitz has suggested that PGD belongs in a new category of Traumatic Stress Reactions along with PTSD, but the *DSM*'s committee prefers to place Bereavement Related Disorder in the category of Adjustment Disorders. This suggests that the condition is primarily a problem of adjustment or coping with the specific stress of bereavement. It is not difficult to support both cases for there is certainly evidence that insecure attachments interfere with adjustment to bereavement, as well as making people more vulnerable to traumatic losses. This said, in the final analysis, it is not coping or trauma that is the root difficulty; the one thing that defines and characterizes PGD is attachment to a loved person. The *DSM-IV-TR* already includes Separation Anxiety Disorder of Childhood and the proposals for *DSM-5* add two more proposed Attachment Disorders, G00 Reactive Attachment Disorder and Disinhibited Social Engagement Disorder. There seems to be little recognition yet by the APA that attachment problems in childhood may persist into adult life despite research that shows this to be so (Dozier, Stovall & Albus, 1999).

As we have seen, much evidence points to insecure attachments as the root cause of PGD and many of the patients with PGD seen by Parkes reported having suffered Separation Anxiety Disorder of Childhood (Parkes, 2006b, pp. 225–235).

Conclusions

As is so often the case, differences between experts often turn out to result from failure of communication or the imprecise use of words. Both of these have taken place in the attempts to establish the complications of grief. Given the complexity of human relationships, the great variation in the causes and circumstances of death, and the wide range of familial, social, and occupational supports to bereaved people, it would be strange if there were only one Bereavement Related Disorder. Empirical studies have, however, enabled us to identify what is probably the most salient of these. PGD is undoubtedly the most common and the most disabling complication of bereavement and it is important that it be recognized and treated. Unfortunately the adoption of the over-inclusive term Complicated Grief Disorder has caused clinicians, who know very well that bereaved people seek help for a variety of psychiatric problems, to muddy the waters by attempting to squeeze a quart into a pint pot. The acceptance that Prigerson's PGD is only one among several complications of grief leaves the door open to the future delineation of others. On the other hand, insistence that it is the only disorder of grieving would close that door.

Colin Murray Parkes, *OBE, MD, FRCPsych, worked closely with the late Dame Cicely Saunders as consultant psychiatrist to St. Christopher's Hospice, in London, England, since its inception in 1966. Dr. Parkes set up the first hospice-based bereavement service and carried out some of the earliest systematic evaluations of hospice care. He worked for 13 years with John Bowlby at the Tavistock Institute of Human Relations and edited two books on the nature of human attachments. Dr. Parkes also serves as the Life President of Cruse Bereavement Care.*

Dr. Parkes is the author of numerous books, including most recently Bereavement: Studies of Grief in Adult Life *(4th edition) with Holly Prigerson, 2010, and* Love and Loss: the Roots of Grief and Its Complications, *published by Routledge. He served as co-editor of* Death and Bereavement across Cultures, *also published by Routledge. Dr. Parkes has also authored numerous publications on psychological aspects of bereavement, amputation of a limb, terminal cancer care, and other life crises. Dr. Parkes is connected with several journals concerned with hospice, palliative care, and bereavement.*

Dr. Parkes has acted as consultant and adviser following both man-made and natural disasters, including the terrorist attacks in Lockerbie and New York, after 9/11. His recent work has focused on traumatic bereavements (with special reference to violent deaths, armed conflict, and the cycle of violence) and on the roots in the attachments of childhood of the psychiatric problems that can follow the loss of attachments in adult life. He was awarded an OBE by Her Majesty The Queen of England for his services to bereaved people in June 1996.

References

Boelen, P. A., de Keijser, J., van den Hout, M. A., & van den Bout, J. (2007). Treatment of complicated grief: A comparison between cognitive-behavioral therapy and supportive counseling. *Journal of Consulting and Clinical Psychology, 75*(2), 277–84.

Boelen, P. A., & Prigerson, H. G. (Pending). Prolonged Grief Disorder as a new psychiatric condition in DSM-5. To be submitted to M. S. Stroebe, H. Schut, & J. van den Bout (Eds.), *Complicated Grief.* New York: Routledge (for publication in 2012).

Childress, A. R., Mozley, P. D., McElgin, W., Fitzgerald, J., Reivich, M., & O'Brien, C. P. (1999). Limbic activation during cue-induced cocaine craving. *American Journal of Psychiatry, 156,* 11–18.

De Mijolla, A. (Ed.). (2005). *International Dictionary of Psychoanalysis.* New York, NY: Macmillan Reference Books.

Dozier, M., Stovall, K. C., & Albus, K. E. (1999). Attachment and psychopathology in adults. In J. Cassidy & P. R. Shaver (Eds.), *Handbook of Attachment: Theory, research and clinical applications.* New York: Guilford.

Dyregrov, K. (2005). Do professionals disempower bereaved people? Grief and social intervention. *Bereavement Care, 24*(1), 7–10.

Gauthier, J., & Marshall, W. L. (1977). Grief: A cognitive behavioural analysis. *Cognitive Therapy and Research, 1,* 39–44.

Gundel, H., O'Connor M. F., Littrel, L., et al. (2003). Functional neuroanatomy of grief: An fMRI study. *American Journal of Psychiatry, 160,* 1946–1953.

Kato, P. M., & Mann, T. (1999). A synthesis of psychological interventions for the bereaved. *Clinical Psychology Review, 19*(3), 275–96.

Klass D., Silverman P. R., & Nickman, S. (Eds.). (1996). *Continuing bonds: New understandings of grief.* Taylor & Francis: Washington DC & London.

Lindemann, E. (1944). The symptomatology and management of acute grief. *American Journal of Psychiatry, 101,* 141.

Maas, L. C., Scott, S. M., Lukas, E., Kaufman, M. J., Weiss, R. D., Daniels, S. L., et al. (1998). Functional magnetic resonance imaging of human brain activation during cue-induced cocaine craving. *American Journal of Psychiatry, 155,* 124–126.

Mawson, D., Marks, I. M., Ramm, L., & Stern, L. S. (1981). Guided mourning for morbid grief: A controlled study. *British Journal of Psychiatry, 138,* 185–193.

O'Connor, M. F., Wellisch, D. K., Stanton, A. L., Eisenberger, M. I., Irwin, M. R., & Lieberman, M. D. (2008). Craving love? Enduring grief activates brain's reward center. *NeuroImage, 42,* 969–972.

Parkes, C. M. (Guest Editor). (2006a). Symposium on Complicated Grief. Introduction and Conclusions. *Omega: Journal of Death and Dying, 52*(1), 1–112.

Parkes, C. M. (2006b). *Love and loss: The roots of grief and its complications.* London, UK: Routledge.

Parkes, C. M., & Prigerson, H. G. (4th edition, 2009). *Bereavement: Studies of grief in adult life.* New York & London: Routledge.

Parkes, C. M., & Weiss, R. S. (1983). *Recovery from bereavement.* New York: Basic Books.

Prigerson, H. G., Maciejewski, P. K., Newsom, J., Reynolds, C. F., III, Frank, E., Bierhals, E. J., Miller, M., et al. (1995). The inventory of complicated grief: A scale to measure maladaptive symptoms of loss. *Psychiatry Research, 59,* 65–79.

Prigerson H. G., Bierhals, A. J., Kasl, S. V., Reynolds, C.F., III, Shear, M. K., Day, N., Beery, L. C., et al. (1997). Traumatic grief as a risk factor for mental and physical morbidity. *American Journal of Psychiatry, 154*(5), 616–23.

Prigerson, H. G., & Maciejewski, P. K. (2006). A call for sound empirical testing and evaluation of criteria for complicated grief proposed for DSM-V. Symposium on Complicated Grief. *Omega: Journal on Death and Dying, 52*(1), 16.

Prigerson, H. G., Vanderwerker, L. C., & Maciejewski, P. K. (2008). Prolonged Grief Disorder: A case for inclusion in DSM-V. Chapter 8 in M. Stroebe, R. Hansson, H. Schut, & W. Stroebe (Eds.), *Handbook of bereavement research and practice: 21st century perspectives.* Washington, D.C.: American Psychological Association Press.

Prigerson, H. G., Horowitz, M. J., Jacobs, S. C., Parkes, C. M., Aslan, M., Goodkin, K., Raphael, B., et al. (2009). Prolonged Grief Disorder: Psychometric validation of criteria proposed for DSM-5 and ICD-11. *PLoS Medicine, 6*(8), e1000121.

Ramsey, R. W. (1979). Bereavement: A behavioral treatment for pathological grief. In P. O. Sioden, S. Bates, & W. S. Dorkens, III (Eds.), *Trends in Behavior Therapy.* New York: Academic Press.

Relf, M. (1998). Involving volunteers in bereavement counselling. *European Journal of Palliative Care, 5*(2), 61–5.

Reynolds, C. F., Miller, M. D., Pasternak, R. E., Frank, E., Perel, J., Cornes, C., Houck, P., et al. (1999). Treatment of bereavement-related major depressive episodes in later life: A controlled study of acute and continuation treatment with nortriptyline and interpersonal psychotherapy. *American Journal of Psychiatry, 156*(2), 202–208.

Shear, K., Frank, E., Houck, P. R., & Reynolds, C. F. (2005). Treatment of complicated grief: A randomized controlled trial. *Journal of the American Medical Association, 293*(21), 2601–7.

Shear, M. K., Simon, N., Wall, M., Zisook, S., Neimeyer, R., Duan, N., Reynolds, C., et al. (2011). Complicated grief and related bereavement-issues for DSM-5. *Depression and Anxiety, 28,* 103–117.

Stroebe, M. S., & Schut, H. (1999). The dual process model of coping with bereavement: Rationale and description. *Death Studies, 23,* 197–224.

Vanderwerker, L. C., Jacobs, S. C., Parkes, C. M., & Prigerson, H. G. (2006). An exploration of associations between separation anxiety in childhood and complicated grief in later life. *Journal of Nervous Mental Disorders, 194*(2), 121–3.

CHAPTER 8

Putting to Rest the Debate Over Grief Counseling

Louis A. Gamino

Two recent books written for a general readership, scholar George Bonanno's (2009) *The Other Side of Sadness: What the New Science of Bereavement Tells Us About Life After Loss* and investigative journalist Ruth Davis Konigsberg's (2011) *The Truth about Grief: The Myth of its Five Stages and the New Science of Loss* have stirred the continuing controversy over the need for grief counseling and its efficacy (or potential harmfulness). While passions on both sides of the debate are readily aroused, an objective review reveals two fundamental findings. First, it is only a minority of bereaved individuals who experience distress of an intensity or duration that warrants professional intervention. Second, when practitioners use sound psychotherapy techniques and empirically-documented treatments to help troubled grievers, results are generally favorable.

The author's intent for this chapter is to summarize what is known from currently available academic sources regarding who needs grief counseling and when grief counseling is most effective. In this chapter, the author draws heavily on material he published previously about these contemporary ethical controversies in grief counseling (Gamino & Ritter, 2009), appropriately updated, in reaching the conclusions presented as consensus. The discussion concludes with two case examples intended to give readers an opportunity to apply the concepts contained in this chapter to everyday clinical work.

WHO NEEDS GRIEF COUNSELING?

In the last decade, Wortman and Silver (2001) revisited the question of whether grievers need to display socially-expected symptoms of sadness and mourning considered mandatory by many professionals and lay persons alike, based on Freud's (1917) enduring notion of grief work. They concluded that not everyone shows intense grief distress and there are some grievers who show few signs of sadness. Commensurately, Stroebe, Hansson, Schut, and

Stroebe (2008a) summarized their review of bereavement research with a similar declaration.

> ...it is important to note that only a minority of bereaved persons suffer from complicated forms of grief and will need the professional help of counselors or therapists. Most bereavements [sic] involve no pathological indications. The majority of bereaved persons will undergo a period of intense suffering and some dysfunction but will be able to deal with their bereavement without professional referral (p. 8).

How do scholars know that most bereaved persons manage to cope or recover without professional help? The work of George Bonanno and colleagues (Bonanno et al. 2002; Bonanno, 2004; Bonanno, Wortman, & Nesse, 2004) was instrumental in introducing the concept of *resilience* to explain how many grievers weather the loss of an important loved one. Drawing on data from a large prospective study of older couples (Bonanno, Boerner & Wortman, 2008), investigators had the advantage of both pre-loss and post-loss measures (at 6 and 18 months afterward) of participants' functioning on a variety of psychometric indices. They found 46% of participants reported low levels of depression before and after the deaths of their loved ones, as well as relatively few grief symptoms during bereavement. They classified this pattern as resilience. Resilient participants were not unmoved by their loss; instead, their emotional perturbations were transient and did not interfere with their ability to function in other life areas, including the capacity for positive affect. Significantly, resilient grievers reported positive memories of their deceased spouse (e.g., talking about or thinking about the decedent) to be comforting, a finding that argued against alternate explanations that they were not strongly attached to their partner or were engaged in defensive denial.

Four other major bereavement patterns were discovered in this prospective data (Bonanno et al. 2002; Bonanno, Wortman, & Nesse, 2004). Participants with *chronic grief* reactions (16%) showed low pre-loss depression levels but exhibited higher post-loss depression and grief symptoms at both measurement periods. In this group, the distress exhibited was due primarily to the cognitive and emotional upheaval surrounding the loss of a healthy spouse. A *common grief* or *recovery pattern* (11%) showed low pre-loss distress levels followed by high post-loss distress at 6 months, yet return to baseline levels at 18 months. A counterintuitive pattern featured high levels of depression pre-loss followed by improvement at both post-loss measurements. Collateral data revealed that individuals with this *depressed-improved* pattern (10%) reported the poorest quality marriages and had spouses who were seriously ill at the time of the pre-bereavement interviews. Finally, some of the sample displayed *chronic depression* (8%) before and after their loss, together with markedly higher grief symptoms. This group's distress was more likely due to enduring emotional difficulties exacerbated by spousal loss. Very few participants showed a *delayed grief* pattern (4%), i.e., low pre-loss depression, no change at 6 months, and a grief reaction at 18 months.

When participants displaying the *chronic grief, recovery, chronic depression,* and *delayed grief* patterns are combined, individuals displaying at least some measurable distress account for 39% of the older couples' sample or, more conservatively, 28% if the recovery group is excluded (Bonanno et al. 2002; Bonanno, Wortman & Nesse, 2004). In an earlier review of the bereavement literature, Bonanno and Kaltman (2001) delineated that only about 15% of bereaved persons show serious disruptions in functioning at 1–2 years following the loss. Clearly, the majority of grievers are resilient or find ways to cope on their own, and only a minority of grievers respond to loss in a manner that requires professional help. In *The Other Side of Sadness,* Bonanno (2009) makes this point repeatedly in an effort to convey to the public that, for most people, the experience of bereavement necessitates neither prolonged suffering nor mandatory counseling.

An interesting small sample study provided a more in-depth look at which grievers elect grief counseling and why (Gamino, Sewell, Hogan, & Mason, 2009–2010). Sixty-nine diverse grievers (recruited from a major teaching hospital where their family member died or referred by their primary care physician) whose loved ones died 12–40 months prior to the study completed psychometric measures of both bereavement *distress* and post-bereavement personal *growth*. In a cluster analysis, three distinct groups emerged: High Grief (high distress—low growth; 23%); High Growth (low distress—high growth; 46%); and Low Impact (low distress—low growth; 30%). These percentages bear a striking resemblance to the data of Bonanno et al. (2002) and Bonanno, Wortman & Nesse (2004). The High Grief group, which endorsed the most distress indicators and showed the poorest adaptation to loss, constituted only 23% of the sample. In contrast, the High Growth group (46%) fared relatively well by activating healthy coping methods (e.g., utilizing social support, displaying optimism, looking for positive outcomes from the experience of bereavement), while the Low Impact group (30%) appeared to grieve in an understated, less expressive fashion.

When it came to seeking professional help among the Gamino et al. (2009–2010) cohort, 50% of the High Grief participants sought psychological or psychiatric care for their grief compared to only 19% each in the High Growth and Low Impact groups. Wanting *relief* from their intense pain and distress appeared to the overriding consideration when High Grief participants sought grief counseling. When High Growth participants elected counseling, they seemed to focus more on personal growth and transformation, whereas Low Impact grievers were more likely to prefer medicinal treatment with antidepressants to grief counseling on the few occasions when they sought professional intervention.

Because empirical studies show that only a minority of bereaved persons are likely to need professional help, Gamino and Ritter (2009) proposed a straightforward screening process intended to identify those grievers who may need grief counseling. Borrowing from and extending the work of Zisook and Lyons (1988–1989) that was later corroborated by Gamino, Sewell, and Easterling (1998), Gamino and Ritter recommend asking a potentially troubled griever two simple questions.

1. *Are you having trouble dealing with the death?* (When positive, they proceed.)
2. *Are you interested in seeing a grief counselor to help with that?*

Bereaved individuals who answer affirmatively to both of these screening questions are likely to be among those who could benefit from grief counseling. The clinical utility of such a screening method received indirect support from the results of Allumbaugh and Hoyt's (1999) meta-analysis of grief therapy studies finding that *self-selected* clients who actively sought professional help for bereavement benefitted the most from counseling. Astute clinicians can augment these subjective indicators with strategic use of risk-factor profiles (cf. Jordan & Neimeyer, 2007; Rando, 1993; Worden, 2009) to identify those bereaved individuals most in need of help who, at the same time, are amenable to mental health intervention.

Once a struggling griever reaches a mental health professional for evaluation, a more detailed assessment process to confirm the need for help was proposed by Shear, Simon, Wall, Zisook, Neimeyer, Duan, et al. (2011) in conjunction with their proposal for a specific diagnostic category of complicated grief. Based on their impressive literature review of the likely component symptoms of complicated grief, they proposed an assessment of five different areas: having trouble accepting the death; finding grief interfering with life; being bothered by images or thoughts of the loved one; avoiding or finding uncomfortable previously enjoyed activities; and feeling cut off from or distant from others. Shear et al. suggest a rating scale for identifying the presence of complicated grief based on whether the bereaved person answers, "Not at all," "Somewhat," or "A lot" to these survey questions. Obviously at this level of inquiry, a therapeutic discussion has already commenced and Shear et al. urge clinicians to be vigilant against either over-diagnosis or under-diagnosis. The two case examples at the end of this chapter illustrate the dynamic nature of this identification and screening process for determining who needs grief counseling.

When Is Grief Counseling Most Effective?

The last decade began with a firestorm of controversy over the effectiveness of grief counseling. First, two meta-analytic reviews suggested that grief counseling generated only minimal to equivocal results. Allumbaugh and Hoyt (1999) found a moderately small but positive treatment effect for individuals receiving grief counseling compared with nontreatment controls, although the expertise of the practitioner (professionals were better than trainees or non-professionals) and treatment modality (individual counseling was better than group) made a difference. When measuring depression and other psychological symptoms, Kato and Mann (1999) found a positive treatment effect so small as to be considered negligible, leading them to conclude that psychological interventions for bereavement are just not effective.

Accelerant to the firestorm came from two reports by Neimeyer (2000; Jordan & Neimeyer, 2003) of unpublished dissertation data compiled by one of his doctoral students asserting, based on an inferential statistical method, that nearly 38% of recipients of grief counseling sustained iatrogenic *worsening* of their problems as a result of grief counseling, an outcome he called "treatment-induced deterioration." Larson and Hoyt (2007) roundly criticized Neimeyer's inferential statistic used to find treatment-induced deterioration and deemed the results spurious. They concluded that there was no compelling evidence that bereaved clients are harmed by grief counseling or that grief counseling, as typically practiced, is less efficacious than other forms of counseling and psychotherapy. They decried the fact that Neimeyer's assertions were cited by other professionals who uncritically accepted his results and promulgated the notion of grief counseling causing harm (cf. Lilienfeld, 2007). Sensationalized reports in the media about the possible harmful effects of grief counseling followed (cf. Begley, 2007; Brody, 2004) even while the scholarly debate continued in a professional forum (Bonanno & Lilienfeld, 2008; Fortner, 2008; Hoyt & Larson, 2008).

Fortunately, results from more comprehensive reviews of the treatment literature began to extinguish the controversy over the efficacy of grief counseling, finding in favor of treatment for certain individuals. Schut, Stroebe, van den Bout, and Terheggen (2001) conducted a broad survey of published studies of bereavement interventions to determine just who might benefit from them. Intervention programs open to all bereaved people (such as support groups for widowed persons) or designed for those thought to be "at risk" for developing complications in grieving, showed only modest improvement at best, and sometimes that was only temporary. However, when reviewing studies of participants who either *sought* help on their own or were *referred* for treatment, outcome effects were still modest yet produced positive and lasting results. Clearly, these latter samples resemble more closely the cohort of grievers that most professional counselors encounter in practice. Schut et al. concluded that, "...the more complicated the grief process appears to be or to become, the better the chances of interventions leading to positive results" (p. 731). The same authors reiterated this conclusion in the latest edition of the *Handbook of Bereavement Research: Advances in Theory and Intervention* (Stroebe, Hansson, Schut, & Stroebe, 2008b; chapter 27).

> Programs are least effective when offered to bereaved persons in general, irrespective of indications that intervention is needed; they are more effective for those who, through screening or assessment, can be regarded as vulnerable, and they are most effective for those who have complicated grief, grief-related depression, or post-traumatic disorders. (p. 597)

Currier, Neimeyer, and Berman (2008) undertook a methodologically meticulous meta-analytic review of 61 controlled outcome studies in order to provide the best possible scientific assessment of the effectiveness of psychotherapeutic intervention for bereaved persons. Each of the surveyed studies compared those receiving grief counseling with a group of bereaved persons who did not receive any active type of intervention (e.g., wait list or delayed treatment control groups). Overall, bereavement interventions showed a small positive effect, outperforming no intervention control conditions when measured immediately following treatment. Follow-up measures were also taken but there was wide variability in the time frame, ranging from 2 weeks to 72 weeks, and no definite effect was found.

Most pertinent to the debate over the efficacy of grief counseling, was Currier et al.'s (2008) results after studies were coded as to whether researchers' interventions were *universal,* i.e., intended for any bereaved person, *selective,* i.e., focused on bereaved individuals thought to be at higher risk of distress based on nuclear family relationship to the deceased or grieving a violent death, or *indicated,* i.e., targeted for participants manifesting bereavement-related difficulties before intervention began. In Currier et al.'s coding scheme, which parallels the classifications employed by Schut et al. (2001), the *indicated* group most closely approximates individuals typically seen in grief counseling practices. Outcomes of interventions with grievers showing poor bereavement adaptation before treatment—generally individuals who were either self-referred or referred by another healthcare professional—showed moderate positive effect sizes both at post-treatment and at follow-up. The authors attest that these results compare favorably with outcome studies of psychotherapy for other difficulties. Currier et al. concluded:

> ...the present comprehensive review documents the relevance of attending to the targeted population and reinforces the growing consensus that psychotherapeutic interventions for bereaved persons can be effective in instances when researchers and clinicians focus on persons who are genuinely in need of help (p. 656).

Additional studies have refined knowledge in the field about what kinds of treatment are most helpful to bereaved persons struggling in the aftermath of an important personal loss. Shear, Frank, Houck, and Reynolds (2005) compared the effectiveness of interpersonal therapy designed for treatment of depression-spectrum disorders (Weissman, Markowitz, & Klerman, 2000) with complicated grief treatment customized to address bereavement in a randomized, controlled trial with 95 bereaved persons assessed to have complicated grief. The complicated grief treatment was designed to focus on both loss-oriented problems and restoration or going on with life, consistent with Stroebe & Schut's (1999; 2010) Dual Process Model of coping with bereavement. Accordingly, for addressing loss-oriented symptoms, they used techniques such as having participants "retell" the story of the death, actively confront or "revisit" their distressing death-related experiences, and connect with the deceased through memory triggers and simulated conversations. For restoration, participants were encouraged to consider what they would like for themselves if their grief were not so intense, define personal life goals, and identify benchmarks that would help them know when they were reaching their goals. While both treatment groups improved, participants in the complicated grief treatment fared better by logging a higher rate of improvement, scoring significantly lower on measures of depression and grief distress, and reporting better work and social adjustment. The work of Shear et al. represents initial steps toward developing treatment protocols for troubled grievers based on contemporary theory and proven therapy methods (Gamino & Ritter, 2009).

Boelen, de Keijser, van den Hout, and van den Bout (2007) compared simple supportive counseling with cognitive-behavioral therapy for 54 mourners with clinically significant levels of complicated grief. Based on the work of Aaron Beck (Beck, Rush, Shaw, & Emery, 1979), the cognitive-behavioral therapy featured both "cognitive restructuring" approaches that challenged negative thought patterns generally and "exposure" strategies that forced participants to tell the story of the loss, progressively confront loss reminders, and elaborate on the implications of the loss. The supportive counseling intervention did not address cognitions and gave no instructions for exposure to loss-related stimuli. The cognitive-behavioral therapy produced more improvement in grief symptoms and general psychopathology than did simple supportive counseling, with the exposure strategies in particular generating more gains. Like Shear et al. (2005), these results suggest that treatment interventions tailored specifically for individuals with complicated grief, using valid methods, have a higher probability of success.

Thus, while the reviews of Currier et al. (2008) and Schut et al. (2001) showed that grief counseling is effective for selected individuals who either *sought* help on their own or were *referred* for treatment, these latter studies (Boelen et al. 2007; Shear et al. 2005) begin to inform practitioners about the critical elements of empirically-supported treatments for bereft individuals having trouble coping. The Dual Process Model of Stroebe and Schut (1999; 2010) appears to be of particular relevance in guiding a bilateral focus on both restoration and grief-oriented dimensions. When attempting to address the pain of the loss, the role of sensitively applied exposure-based strategies is necessary.

A final note about the efficacy of grief counseling pertains to the advice of Gamino and Ritter (2009) that bereaved individuals seek service from practitioners with demonstrated *death competence*—specialized skill in tolerating and managing clients' problems related to dying, death, and bereavement. In all forms of psychotherapy, a positive outcome is a product of both provider and client variables (cf. Lambert, 2004). Providers possessing death competence are in the strongest position to counsel the bereaved in a sensitive manner tailored to the specific needs of a given clinical situation and incorporating the latest pertinent research findings. Gamino and Ritter (in press) argued for the importance of death competence in an in-depth case study of the only participant from an earlier published report who did *not* find grief counseling helpful (Gamino et al. 2009–2010; 10 of 11 participants or 91% who sought grief counseling found it to be beneficial). They concluded that the provider lacked death competence needed for grief counseling, resulting in "empathic failure" (cf. Neimeyer & Jordan, 2002).

Two Case Examples
Case A:

"Gina" was a white widow in her late 50s, self-referred for grief counseling, whose question to the therapist following the death of her husband approximately one year prior was, "Am I normal?" She had no history of mental health treatment in her life, but family members had urged her to come for counseling. Gina was unsure whether she needed professional help. She had thought about a support group, but had never attended one.

Gina described her 39 years of marriage as "magical" because, "Nobody ever loved me the way he did; it was unconditional." Her husband was a Vietnam-era veteran with a number of different physical ailments related to Agent Orange exposure, so he was used to being a stoic sufferer. Gina believes that is the reason why he did not complain about any lung symptoms until he was so short of breath that he could not function. Stage IV lung cancer was diagnosed and he lived only 6 weeks thereafter, spending his last 48 hours in a nursing home. She found his death "shocking" because, "I thought he would get through it."

Gina was born when her mother was only 17. When her father died young, her mother began a "wild" period of reclaiming her adolescence so Gina was always the "strong one" for her younger siblings. After her husband's death, she had tried to be a strong and comforting presence to others, especially her three children. She had some crying spells and some transient anxiety where she did not want to leave the house, but otherwise had been able to function. She made a number of sensible business decisions related to the estate, such as paying off debts and burial costs, remodeling the house for "retirement," and positioning *herself financially to have steady income from his death benefits. Gina worked one day a week in a retail setting, as a diversion, and enjoyed interacting with the public.*

In the case of "Gina," the grief counselor's impression was that she closely resembled what Bonanno (2009) described from his research as a *resilient* griever, or what Gamino et al. (2009–2010) called a *low-impact* griever. Her distress over the loss of her cherished husband and the associated emotional perturbations, while present, were transient and did not prevent her from functioning as a mother, as an employee, or as executrix of his estate. At approximately 12 months after her husband's death, Gina seemed to be doing relatively well and much of the counselor's efforts went toward normalization of her reactions and psycho-education about grief. These interventions were consistent with Worden's (2009) ideas about facilitating uncomplicated grief. The initial session ended with affirmation by the counselor that, indeed, Gina appeared to be "normal" for a widow in her position. The counselor provided additional information about community-based support groups and extended an open invitation to return if help was needed in the future, but scheduled no subsequent appointments.

Gina's responses at the conclusion of the meeting indicated that the single session had been useful and validating for her. She intended to reassure her family that she was doing "okay" and would give some thought to attending a support group if she felt the need. The counselor in this scenario appeared to operate in an ethical manner by carefully evaluating Gina's case, making even an intake session beneficial for her, and "doing no harm" (i.e., non-malificence; cf. Beauchamp & Childress, 2008; Gamino & Ritter, 2009) by not recommending a course of grief counseling for a widow doing well enough without it. Instead, Gina clearly seems to be among the majority of grievers who do not need grief counseling.

Returning to the two screening questions proposed by Gamino and Ritter (2009) to identify those individuals who may actually need grief counseling, Gina seemed to answer positively the first question of "having trouble dealing with the death" of her husband. While she had enough doubt about seeking professional help that she agreed to an initial appointment to find out for certain, the balance of the consultation seemed to prove that she was resilient enough to make her way without grief counseling.

Case B:

"Bonny" was a white female in her middle 60s, self-referred for mental health evaluation after the death of her husband approximately three months earlier. She reported "crying all day," isolating herself from friends, staying home because there she felt "closer" to her deceased husband, and feeling sentimental when she heard a song or anything that reminded her of him. She felt depressed. Her children expressed concern that she was not doing well and wanted her to "get on with life" so Bonny wondered about her reactions; were they " normal?" She first went to a counselor associated with the funeral home but "did not like him" and then went to a support group meeting but decided that it was "not for me."

Bonny grew up with a likeable but alcoholic father and a screaming mother who was "not close to us." Everyone in the family smoked, including Bonny, although she had quit. Her father and siblings died of emphysema and Bonny had a mild case as well. Bonny was a recovered alcoholic who had been sober for 18 years with the help of Alcoholics Anonymous. When Bonny married her deceased husband, she already had three children from two previous marriages. He adopted her children, they had a fourth child, and stayed together almost 40 years until his death. He did not drink even when she did.

Bonny's husband was a disabled Vietnam-era veteran with Agent Orange exposure and numerous health problems. In the last few months before his death, he became uncharacteristically "obsessive" about his medicines and unusually affectionate toward her. The day he died, her husband was short of breath and became very quiet. When she tried to help, he said, "Leave me alone, I don't feel good." So Bonny went to take a shower and when she returned, he was already dead. She had tremendous guilt over not being with him when he died and she also felt a lot of anger that "he left me and I'm all by myself with no one to talk to."

In the case of "Bonny," her husband's death was much more recent (only three months) and her bereavement distress more acute, perhaps still in the process of "peaking" at around the six-month mark post-loss (cf. Bonanno et al. 2002; Bonanno, 2004). From a statistical perspective, it may have been too early in Bonny's bereavement trajectory to differentiate whether she was on a course similar to grievers who demonstrate a *recovery* pattern wherein distress starts to decline at about six months post-loss or a *chronic grief* pattern where distress persists well beyond the first year.

From a clinical perspective, Bonny evidenced a number of worrisome signs indicating she may, indeed, be a candidate for grief counseling. In addition to her complaints of depression symptoms, she reported potentially problematic indicators such as the unremitting guilt over somehow failing her husband by not being there at the moment of his death. She also felt intense anger over his departure from her life, together with a less-than-logical inclination to blame him for leaving her. The overall "Gestalt" of her clinical presentation resembled the High Grief group described by Gamino et al. (2009–2010) wherein bereavement distress is significant and grievers seek relief from their intense pain. Clearly, she answered affirmatively the first screening question of having trouble dealing with the death of her husband.

Recalling that Bonny had reached out twice already for help, once from the mortuary-based counselor and once from a support group, she seemed more intent on seeking help from professional grief counseling. At the conclusion of the first interview, she readily accepted an offer of continuing care from the grief counselor, recognizing that she needed help to cope with her bereavement. Confirming the likely value of continuing counseling for Bonny was the fact that, unlike her first attempt to get help from a counselor, she felt a positive "connection" with the second clinician that gave her hope that her condition could improve. Thus, Bonny endorsed the second question of the two-part screening—wanting grief counseling to help with her bereavement distress (Gamino & Ritter, 2009).

Subsequently, Bonny attended six additional sessions of grief counseling that spanned a time interval of 13 months after her husband's death. Despite making some progress in accepting the finality of his death and finding solace in her religious beliefs, she continued to have trouble coping and her grief trajectory seemed to fall more in line with *chronic grief*. Often, she felt it would be better to die and be with her deceased husband in the afterlife, particularly because it was her perception that no one in her life now, even her children, truly cared what happened to her. Her depression symptoms persisted to the point that she decided to ask her doctor for antidepressant medication. Additional history-taking revealed that she was angry with her husband not only for leaving her by dying but also for the dearth of sexual intimacy in their marriage over the last several years due to his multiple health problems.

With the counselor's encouragement, Bonny took constructive steps of reaching out to a widowed friend from whom she took inspiration (e.g., "If she can do it, I can do it…"), communicating more with one son who was most attentive, and journaling about her grief and anger. Gradually, with these steps and with the catharsis of the therapy sessions, she began to release some of the negative emotion she was carrying. She felt better taking an antidepressant. Impressively, at the one-year anniversary of her husband's death, Bonny spontaneously organized a celebration of his life by having a family barbeque where they told humorous stories about her husband and lit a lantern in his memory. She found these rituals comforting.

By 13 months post-loss, Bonny appeared to show a *recovery* trajectory that was facilitated by the grief counseling. The effectiveness of the grief counseling for her was apparent from her diminishing distress, her improved self-confidence, and by an increasingly hopeful attitude about the future that there may yet be another chapter of life beyond the years with her deceased husband. In particular, reading and processing the emotional pain expressed in her journal entries during the grief counseling sessions introduced an "exposure" element to the treatment (Boelen et al. 2007). Also, the counselor appeared to maintain a bilateral focus on both grief-oriented and restoration-oriented endeavors suggested by the dual process model (Stroebe & Schut, 1999, 2010) and shown to be effective by Shear et al. (2005). Other researchers (Lund, Caserta, Utz, & de Vries, 2010) are developing intervention strategies based on the dual process model although, because they have been applied only to a general population of grievers rather than those displaying complicated grief, their work remains preliminary.

Summary

The continuing controversies over the need for grief counseling and questions about its effectiveness appear to be a debate waged more in popular media than in scholarly circles. Review of the scientific literature bears out that most bereaved persons find ways to cope with loss without requiring professional help but, when grief counseling is needed, empirically-supported treatment methods are generally effective. This consensus is summarized by Gamino and Ritter (2009, p. 258).

> "Grief counseling practiced by competent professionals can help those individuals struggling to accommodate to their loss and is especially helpful for those who self-identify their need or whose personal history and circumstances make it even more difficult than usual to cope with their loss."

Louis A. Gamino, *PhD, ABPP, FT,* is a diplomate in clinical psychology on staff with Scott & White Healthcare® in Temple, TX. Dr. Gamino is also professor of psychiatry and behavioral science, Texas A&M University Health Science Center College of Medicine. His practice subspecialty is treatment of complicated grief. In recognition of excellence in clinical care of the dying and the bereaved, Dr. Gamino was the 2008 recipient of the Clinical Practice Award given by the Association for Death Education and Counseling (ADEC). Dr. Gamino is co-author, with Hal Ritter, Jr., of a full-length textbook, Ethical Practice in Grief Counseling *(2009, Springer Publishing Company).* Together with Ann Cooney, he is co-author of When Your Baby Dies Through Miscarriage or Stillbirth *(2002, Augsburg Fortress).* Dr. Gamino is former editor of The Forum, *a newsletter published by ADEC. He is also chair of the ADEC Ethics Committee.*

REFERENCES

Allumbaugh, D. L., & Hoyt, W. T. (1999). Effectiveness of grief therapy: A meta-analysis. *Journal of Consulting Psychology, 46,* 370–380.

Beauchamp, T. L., & Childress, J. F. (2008). *Principles of biomedical ethics* (6th Ed.). New York: Oxford University Press.

Beck, A. T., Rush, A. J., Shaw, B. F., & Emery, G. (1979). *Cognitive therapy of depression.* New York: Guilford.

Boelen, P. A., de Keijser, J., van den Hout, M. A., & van den Bout, J. (2007). Treatment of complicated grief: A comparison between cognitive-behavioral therapy and supportive counseling. *Journal of Consulting and Clinical Psychology, 75,* 277–284.

Begley, S. (2007, June 18). Get shrunk at your own risk. *Newsweek,* p. 49.

Bonanno, G. A. (2004). Loss, trauma and human resilience: Have we underestimated the human capacity to thrive after extremely aversive events? *American Psychologist, 59,* 20–28.

Bonanno, G. A. (2009). *The other side of sadness: What the new science of bereavement tells us about life after loss.* New York: Basic.

Bonanno, G. A., Boerner, K., & Wortman, C. B. (2008). Trajectories of grieving. In M. Stroebe, R. O. Hansson, H. Schut, & W. Stroebe (Eds.), *Handbook of bereavement research and practice: Advances in theory and intervention* (pp. 287–307). Washington, DC: American Psychological Association.

Bonanno, G. A., & Kaltman, S. (2001). The varieties of grief experience. *Clinical Psychology Review, 21,* 705–734.

Bonanno, G. A., & Lilienfeld, S. O. (2008). Let's be realistic: When grief counseling is effective and when it's not. *Professional Psychology: Research and Practice, 39,* 377–378.

Bonanno, G. A., Wortman, C. B., Lehman, D. R., Tweed, R. G., Haring, M., Sonnega, J., Carr, D., et al. (2002). Resilience to loss and chronic grief: A prospective study from preloss to 18-months postloss. *Journal of Personality and Social Psychology, 83,* 1150–1164.

Bonanno, G. A., Wortman, C. B., & Nesse, R. M. (2004). Prospective patterns of resilience and maladjustment during widowhood. *Psychology and Aging, 19,* 260–271.

Brody, J. E. (2004, January 27). Often, time beats therapy for treating grief. *The New York Times,* p. F7.

Currier, J. M., Neimeyer, R. A., & Berman, J. S. (2008). The effectiveness of psychotherapeutic interventions for bereaved persons: A comprehensive quantitative review. *Psychological Bulletin, 134,* 648–661.

Fortner, B. V. (2008). Stemming the TIDE: A correction of Fortner (1999) and a clarification of Larson and Hoyt (2007). *Professional Psychology: Research and Practice, 39,* 379–380.

Freud, S. (1957). Mourning and melancholia. In J. Strachey (Ed. and Trans.), *The standard edition of the complete psychological works of Sigmund Freud* (Vol. 14; pp. 239–260). London: Hogarth. (Original work published 1917).

Gamino, L. A., & Ritter, R. H., Jr., (in press). Death competence: An ethical imperative. *Death Studies.*

Gamino, L. A., & Ritter, R. H., Jr., (2009). *Ethical Practice in Grief Counseling.* New York: Springer Publishing.

Gamino, L. A., Sewell, K. W., & Easterling, L. W. (1998). Scott & White Grief Study: An empirical test of predictors of intensified mourning. *Death Studies, 22,* 333–355.

Gamino, L. A., Sewell, K. W., Hogan, N. S., & Mason, S. L. (2009-2010). Who needs grief counseling? A report from the Scott & White Grief Study, *Omega: Journal of Death and Dying, 60,* 199–223.

Hoyt, W. T., & Larson, D. G. (2008). A realistic approach to drawing conclusions from the scientific literature: Response to Bonanno and Lilienfeld (2008). *Professional Psychology: Research and Practice, 39*, 378–379.

Jordan, J. R., & Neimeyer, R. A. (2003). Does grief counseling work? *Death Studies, 27*, 765–786.

Jordan, J. R., & Neimeyer, R. A. (2007). Historical and contemporary perspectives on assessment and intervention. In D. Balk, C. Wogrin, G. Thornton, & D. Meagher (Eds.), *Handbook of thanatology: The essential body of knowledge for the study of death, dying and bereavement* (pp. 213–225). Northbrook, IL: Association for Death Education and Counseling, the Thanatology Association.

Kato, P. M., & Mann, T. (1999). A synthesis of psychological interventions for the bereaved. *Clinical Psychology Review, 19*, 275–296.

Konigsberg, R. D. (2011). *The truth about grief: The myth of its five stages and the new science of loss.* New York: Simon & Schuster.

Lambert, M. J. (2004). *Bergin and Garfield's handbook of psychotherapy and behavior change* (5th ed.). New York: Wiley.

Larson, D. G., & Hoyt, W. T. (2007). What has become of grief counseling? An evaluation of the empirical foundations of the new pessimism. *Professional Psychology: Research and Practice, 38*, 347–355.

Lilienfeld, S. O. (2007). Psychological treatments that cause harm. *Perspectives on Psychological Science, 2*, 53–70.

Lund, D., Caserta, M., Utz, R., & de Vries, B. (2010). Experiences and early coping of bereaved spouses/partners in an intervention based on the Dual Process Model (DPM). *Omega: Journal of Death and Dying, 61*, 291–313.

Neimeyer, R. A. (1998). *Lessons of loss: A guide to coping.* New York: McGraw Hill.

Neimeyer, R. A. (2000). Searching for the meaning of meaning: Grief therapy and the process of reconstruction. *Death Studies, 24*, 541–558.

Neimeyer, R. A., & Jordan, J. R. (2002). Disenfranchisement as empathic failure: Grief therapy and the co-construction of meaning. In K. J. Doka (Ed.), *Disenfranchised grief* (pp. 95–117). Champaign, IL: Research Press.

Rando, T. A. (1993). *Treatment of complicated mourning*. Champaign, IL: Research Press.

Schut, H., Stroebe, M. S., van den Bout, J., & Terheggen, M. (2001). The efficacy of bereavement interventions: Determining who benefits. In M.S. Stroebe, R.O. Hansson, W. Stroebe, & H. Schut (Eds.), *Handbook of bereavement research: Consequences, coping and care* (pp. 705–737). Washington, DC: American Psychological Association.

Shear, K., Frank, E., Houck, P. R., & Reynolds, C. F. (2005). Treatment of complicated grief: A randomized controlled trial. *The Journal of the American Medical Association, 293,* 2601–2608.

Shear, M. K., Simon, N., Wall, M., Zisook, S., Neimeyer, R. A., Duan, N., Reynolds, C., et al. (2011). Complicated grief and related bereavement issues for DSM-5. *Depression and Anxiety, 28,* 103–117.

Stroebe, M. S., Hansson, R. O., Schut, H., & Stroebe, W. (2008a). Bereavement research: Contemporary perspectives. In M. Stroebe, R. O. Hansson, H. Schut, & W. Stroebe (Eds.), *Handbook of bereavement research and practice: Advances in theory and intervention* (pp. 3–25). Washington, DC: American Psychological Association.

Stroebe, M. S., Hansson, R. O., Schut, H., & Stroebe, W. (2008b). Bereavement research: 21st-century prospects. In M. Stroebe, R. O. Hansson, H. Schut, & W. Stroebe (Eds.), *Handbook of bereavement research and practice: Advances in theory and intervention* (pp. 577–603). Washington, DC: American Psychological Association.

Stroebe, M., & Schut, H. (1999). The Dual Process Model of coping with bereavement: Rationale and description. *Death Studies, 23,* 197–224.

Stroebe, M., & Schut, H. (2010). The Dual Process Model of coping with bereavement: A decade on. *Omega: Journal of Death and Dying, 61,* 289–2010.

Weissman, M. M., Markowitz, J. C., & Klerman, G. L. (2000). *Comprehensive guide to interpersonal psychotherapy*. New York: Basic.

Worden, J. W. (2009). *Grief counseling and grief therapy* (4th ed.). New York: Springer.

Wortman, C. B., & Silver, R. C. (2001). The myths of coping with loss revisited. In M. S. Stroebe, R. O. Hansson, W. Stroebe, & H. Schut (Eds.), *Handbook of bereavement research: Consequences, coping and care* (pp. 405–429). Washington, DC: American Psychological Association.

Zisook, S., & Lyons, L. (1988–1989). Bereavement and unresolved grief in psychiatric outpatients. *Omega: Journal of Death and Dying, 20,* 43–58.

CHAPTER 9

From *Stage Follower* to *Stage Manager*: Contemporary Directions in Bereavement Care

Robert A. Neimeyer

There was a time, not all that long ago, when clinical educators, healthcare professionals, and most of the bereaved themselves took comfort in what was presumed to be the predictability of grieving. Under broadly normal circumstances (as in the case of anticipated loss through illness), the dominant model of mourning conjured a journey through bereavement with identifiable way-stations. These were helpfully labeled *denial* (alluding to the protective distancing from the hard reality of actual or pending loss), *anger* (a form of protest against this ominous reality), *bargaining* (a sort of "magical thinking" that attempted to reverse the seemingly impossible state of affairs), *depression* (signaling acquiescence to this fact and the beginning of "letting go"), and finally, at least for the fortunate few, *acceptance* (reflecting accommodation of the loss with greater equanimity) (Kübler-Ross, 1969). Granted, even such pioneering figures as Freud and Lindemann recognized that grieving did not necessarily go smoothly, and accordingly generations of psychologists, social workers, and especially physicians informally diagnosed the presumed "pathologies" of grieving, often vaguely understood as a failure to "withdraw emotional energy from the deceased" in order to invest it elsewhere, or alternatively as resistance against experiencing and expressing the pain of loss altogether (Neimeyer & Gamino, 2006). Nonetheless, a focus on stage models of grieving continued to dominate both professional education in the field (Downe-Wambolt & Tamlyn, 1997) and lay understandings of grief (Dennis, in press) through the 20th century.

As this book attests, however, much has changed in 21st-century bereavement studies. This chapter summarizes recent research that both challenges and refines phase models of adaptation to bereavement, and then offers a synthesis of major trends in contemporary grief research, with an emphasis on their implications for practice. In doing so I will also develop an alternative metaphor for understanding the human engagement with loss, one that casts both the bereaved and the professionals who help them in more active roles than stage-like conceptions of grieving suggest.

Stages of Grief: Some Recent Evidence

Despite the popularity and intuitive appeal of stage models of grief, only a few attempts have been made to empirically test their merits. The most prominent of these was conducted by Maciejewski and colleagues (Maciejewski, Zhang, Block, & Prigerson, 2007), who tested a phasic model of grief based on the work of Jacobs (Jacobs, 1993). Much like Kübler-Ross (1969), Jacobs presumed that normal grief is initially characterized by disbelief (which gradually decreases over time); followed by yearning, anger, and depression (which show distinct peaks in the order presented); and concludes with acceptance (which gradually increases over time).

To test this theory, Maciejewski and his co-workers (2007) examined patterns of change in grief experiences across the first two years of bereavement, mostly in older adults grieving the loss of a spouse by natural causes. Analyses revealed that participants' predominant response, regardless of the amount of time since loss, was *acceptance*—a finding that was inconsistent with stage theory. However, Maciejewski and colleagues (2007) did find that indicators of each stage reached their respective maximum values in a sequence that was in line with stage theory (i.e., first disbelief, then yearning, then anger, then depression and finally acceptance), even if the absolute magnitude of the indicator of each of these states was discrepant with a stage-based conceptualization.

To shed further light on this issue, Jason Holland and I conducted a further study to examine the relation between time since loss and several grief indicators, similar to the ones tested previously by Maciejewski and colleagues. To do so, we recruited a large, ethnically diverse sample of over 440 young adults in the first two years of bereavement who experienced losses by natural causes (both sudden and anticipated) as well as nearly 175 who lost loved ones by violent causes (including homicide, suicide, and fatal accidents) (J. Holland & Neimeyer, 2010). This investigation also considered how a meaning-oriented perspective, which stresses the importance of finding meaning and making sense of loss, might enhance our understanding of the grief experiences associated with stage theories. In contrast to such theories, this constructivist approach conceptualizes grief as a highly individualized process that is largely influenced by the personal meanings people ascribe to a loss (Neimeyer, 2001; Neimeyer & Sands, 2011). In the Holland and Neimeyer (2010) study, the extent to which a participant had made sense of a loss was examined side-by-side with other grief indicators, to allow for a comparison of patterns across different durations of time since loss.

What support did this large-sample study provide for a stage theory of grieving? In a phrase, very little. In general, in the natural death cohort (the one more closely resembling Maciejewski's sample), all of the indicators of grief distress tended to rise and fall as a group, in an inverse relationship to their level of acceptance of the loss. However, acceptance predominated across the entire course of two years of bereavement, from the earliest weeks. Seemingly, as suggested by Bonanno, the average survivor losing a loved one to illness showed considerable resilience (Bonanno, 2004), with relatively modest levels of yearning and depression, very little evidence of anger or denial, and high levels of acceptance across the two years studied. There was some suggestion that distress was mitigated by the passage of time for this group, although the ability of the survivor to "make sense" of the loss in spiritual, secular, or practical terms was a far more robust predictor of adjustment than the number of months since the death, a point to which we will return later.

The situation was quite different with the violent death group, however. For those whose loved ones died by homicide, suicide, and fatal accident, disbelief actually eclipsed other grief indicators in the earliest weeks following the loss. Anger and depression remained predominant in early months, possibly interfering with processing of attachment-related emotions such as yearning in this tragically bereaved population. Although grief-related distress was much more marked and persistent for these violently bereaved individuals, acceptance still emerged as the dominant response among individuals bereaved for a longer period of time, possibly indicating that most grievers are fairly resilient even in the face of objectively traumatic loss. In general, however, adaptation appeared more chaotic over a longer span of time, with an ongoing struggle to find meaning or acceptance regarding the loss persisting through the first half-year, as disbelief gradually declined. Still, little by way of qualitatively different stages of grief was observed over time, beyond some indication of an "anniversary effect" reflected in an increase in distress for participants approaching the 24-month point in their bereavement.

Given the limited support for a stage-like conception of grieving offered by these findings as well as those of Maciejewski and colleagues, it is worth considering why a phasic model of grief continues to hold such appeal for the general public, and, to a lesser extent, for the professionals who work with them—perhaps especially those who have not specialized in grief therapy. One answer might be that human beings are inveterate seekers of patterns to organize the flux of experience in a fashion that enhances their sense of prediction and control (Kelly, 1955). Certainly such motivation could be greatly enhanced by the cognitive, emotional, and social turmoil occasioned by the death of a loved one, when the promise of a predictable "roadmap" through the terrain of loss would be welcomed by many of the bereaved.

A second, and perhaps still more basic, reason that a sequential plotting of grief responses is difficult to resist, is that it may correspond to the fundamental narrative structure of much of human thought (Fireman, McVay, & Flanagan, 2003; Neimeyer, van Dyke, & Pennebaker, 2009), which seeks to "tell a good story" by arranging events in terms of a meaningful beginning, middle, and end, moving from an early perturbation of the plot through various obstacles to the achievement of valued goals (Bruner, 1990; Neimeyer & Levitt, 2000).

A further and related factor could be that stage theory suggests a particular *kind* of narrative structure to grieving, one in which the protagonist is thrust into what Joseph Campbell described as *the hero's journey*. This archetypal story appears across widely varying cultures, in which the hero is called forth from the normal world to face and overcome a series of great trials, ultimately to return triumphant with special knowledge or a special gift to bestow on others (Campbell, 1988). This epic narrative structure is easily enough seen in popular depictions of "the griever's journey," which like Campbell's "monomyth" commonly depict the protagonist's psychospiritual quest as he or she crosses a liminal threshold into an unknown and dangerous world. Typically, the protagonist undergoes a personal metamorphosis as the journey proceeds, before reentering the known world transformed and bearing a special boon—such as wisdom or compassion—to confer on his or her fellows. In this view, the seemingly magnetic draw of a stage-like depiction of grieving that begins with a disorienting separation from the "normal," pre-bereavement world, and that progresses heroically through a series of clearly marked emotional trials before eventuating in a triumphant stage of acceptance, recovery, or symbolic return, may owe more to its compelling coherence with a seemingly universal narrative structure than to its objective accuracy. Simply stated, stage theory may have functioned as the bereavement field's own cultural "monomyth."

FROM *STAGE FOLLOWER* TO *STAGE MANAGER*: TOWARD ACTIVE MODELS OF GRIEVING

If existing data lend little support to a view of mourners as following discernable stages of grief, what alternative models might be considered? In the remainder of this brief chapter I argue that a model of grievers as *stage followers* could be usefully supplanted by one of survivors as *stage managers*, actively marshaling resources for "performing" life in the wake of loss, both in the "backstage" of their personal emotions, thoughts, prayers, and private actions, and on the "front stage" of the social world. In the theatrical profession the role of stage managers is a broad one, as they function as the essential link between all branches of company, serving particularly critical roles in the recruitment of actors, organization of rehearsals, coordination of activity onstage, managing changes of scenery, and dealing with emergencies. Likewise, in the world of grief, where individuals and families are commonly called on to enact new roles under difficult circumstances, the metaphor of stage management implies that grievers play their parts in concert with others, recruit support for a challenging real-life drama, typically "try out" new parts as they move toward greater competency over time, muster efforts toward a successful performance on the stage of the social world, and negotiate any number of unforeseen complications in the course of doing so. Of course, like any metaphor, this one highlights certain aspects of grieving (such as personal and social activities that promote or impede performance) at the expense of others (such as the biological and broadly cultural factors involved in loss adaptation). But my intent here is simply to emphasize the extent to which grieving can be viewed as an active, and often artful, effort to marshal personal and social resources toward the performance of a new role—a conception that carries useful implications for practicing grief therapists.

Rewriting the Script: Meaning Reconstruction in the Wake of Loss

As suggested above, one of the appeals of traditional stage theory is that it provides a sort of "through line" that orients mourners to the psychological drama of bereavement, even if it fails to offer a very persuasive or compelling account of the changing plot structure of their post-loss lives. Indeed, although resilient survivors are able to reinstate the basic story lines or "self narratives" (Neimeyer, 2004) that underpin their sense of identity after a transient disruption, many others feel thrown into an alien world without a script to tell them who they now are, and what they must now do. Especially when losses are traumatic, even the core themes of predictability and justice that shore up their "assumptive world" (Janoff-Bulman & Berger, 2000) may be called into question, and survivors may find that the comic, romantic, heroic, or adventurous performance in which they were engaged has suddenly turned tragic—or worse, into a theater of the absurd. Stated less metaphorically, profound loss can challenge the basic framework of meaning on which we rely to understand what we have suffered, as well as the significance of our lives in its wake.

In recent years a *meaning reconstruction* approach to grief (Neimeyer, 2001) has explored just this conception, yielding numerous studies that document the role of meaning making in accommodating to loss, and arguing for the relevance of narrative, dramatic, and expressive methods that help people make sense of their bereavement in affirmative ways. For example, studies indicate that being able to make sense of the tragic deaths of their children in personal or practical terms accounts for greatly more of the adaptation of bereaved parents than does the passage of time, the gender of the parent, or even whether their child died as a result of disease or violence (Keesee, Currier, & Neimeyer, 2008). The most helpful themes in their sense-making efforts seem to be those that focus on spiritual meanings and their child being beyond suffering (Lichtenthal, Currier, Neimeyer, & Keesee, 2010). Similarly, among young adults sense-making functions as a powerful mediator of the impact of different modes of death, accounting for essentially all of the difference in complicated grief symptoms between those bereaved by anticipated and sudden natural deaths, as well as between these forms of loss and those resulting from suicide, homicide, and fatal accident (Currier, Holland, & Neimeyer, 2006). In the case of spousal bereavement in later life, longitudinal research demonstrates that a futile search for meaning in the first 6 months of loss predicts more intense grief and depression at 18 and 48 months post-loss, whereas the ability to find meaning in the loss early in bereavement predicts widows' and widowers' levels of well-being, pride, and satisfaction with their lives a full four years later (Coleman & Neimeyer, 2010). Finally, recent research provides evidence that bereaved persons who are able to integrate the loss experience into their meaning systems are better able to preserve aspects of their assumptive world centering on the benevolence of the universe and their own self-worth, and that those who move toward greater integration over time show corresponding reductions in their levels of prolonged grief symptomatology (J. M. Holland, Currier, Coleman, & Neimeyer, 2010). These results support the argument that adaptive grieving entails reaffirming or reconstructing a world of meaning that has been challenged by loss (Neimeyer, 2002, 2006), an outcome to which grief therapy is well positioned to make an important contribution.

What sorts of strategies might assist practicing therapists with this goal? One answer would be utilizing existing resources available to the client such as spiritual or religious beliefs that confer meaning on the loss (Burke & Neimeyer, 2011), or in some cases, that provide elaborate scripting for the difficult performance of mourning, as in orthodox Jewish rituals for grieving that prescribe traditional means of expressing grief during defined periods, giving and receiving consolation, etc. (Heilman, 2002). When such long-term or even short-term supports prove unavailable or unreliable, however, counselors can join their clients in the construction of personal rituals to honor their unique losses (Lewis & Hoy, 2011), especially when such losses are disenfranchised (Doka, 2002) and hence deritualized within the griever's culture.

At a process level, therapists can assist clients in rewriting the script of the loss and the life it ushers in using any of numerous meaning-oriented procedures, ranging from various conversational practices to more formal written narratives (Neimeyer, 2002). For example, the *meaning reconstruction interview* begins with various *entry questions* to elicit a "thick description" of the story of the death itself, progresses to several *experiencing questions* to foster a more emotional, sensory engagement with the loss, moves to *explanation questions* that explicitly engage issues of meaning, and concludes with a set of *elaboration questions* to prompt further reflective processing of the implications of the loss for the client's present and future.

Clinician's Toolbox: Meaning Reconstruction Interview

Entry Questions
- What experience of death or loss would you like to explore?
- What do you recall about how you responded to the event at the time?
- How did your feelings about it change over time?
- How did others in your life at that time respond to the loss? To your reactions to it?
- Who were you as a person, developmentally, at the time of the loss?

Experiencing Questions
- Close your eyes and visualize a scene connected with your loss (take a few moments to find the image). Who or what is in the focus of your attention? Who is on the periphery? What is happening? If you are in the picture, where are you placed?
- What feelings, if any, do you notice in your body as you vivify this loss? What form do these take? Is there movement associated with them? If so, in what direction? If not, is there any blockage of this movement?
- What was the most emotionally significant part of the experience to you?

Explanation Questions
- How did you make sense of the death or loss at the time?
- How do you interpret the loss now?
- What philosophical or spiritual beliefs contributed to your adjustment to this loss? How were they affected by it, in turn?
- Are there ways in which this loss disrupted the continuity of your life story? How, across time, have your dealt with this?

Elaboration Questions
- How has this experience affected your sense of priorities?
- How has this experience affected your view of yourself or your world?
- What lessons about loving has this person or this loss taught you?
- How would your life be different if this person had lived/this loss did not occur?
- What metaphor or image would you use to symbolize your grief over this loss?
- Are there any steps that you could take that would be helpful or healing now?

A responsive therapist will select, adapt, and invent questions that are relevant to the client's unique loss and idiosyncratic mode of processing, with the goal of helping him or her explore and consolidate hopeful appraisals of the experience and the revised life script that it may require.

Other meaning-enhancing interventions may take a *journaling* form, such as encouraging clients to do a cathartic "free write" about the death, compose a letter that offers a helpful perspective to a hypothetical friend who suffered a loss parallel to the client's own, or write about the unsought benefits of the experience repeatedly across a week of intensive engagement with the memory of the death. The developing database supporting such procedures provides encouragement for their more widespread utilization and creative extension (Lichtenthal & Cruess, 2010; Wagner, Knaevelsrud, & Maercker, 2006). The Clinician's Toolbox below offers some evidence-based guidelines for freeform journaling about loss (Neimeyer et al., 2009), which can be modified to accommodate specific instructional sets, such as to focus on the "silver lining" in the loss or on its hidden lessons, to enhance its power or relevance for a given client.

Clinician's Toolbox: **Guidelines for Therapeutic Journals**
- Find a private place where you will not be interrupted
- Focus on one of the more traumatic experiences of your life
- Write about those aspects that are most difficult to acknowledge
- Shift between external event and your deepest thoughts and feelings
- Abandon a concern with grammar and syntax: Write only for yourself
- Write 20 minutes a day, for at least four days
- Schedule a "transitional activity" to return to life as usual
- Have a support person or professional available in case of need

Note: If used as an adjunct to therapy, integrate into session through reading selected passages aloud, rather than the therapist reading between sessions.

Managing Distress: Modulating Negative Emotion

As in the theater, grieving entails the skillful modulation of emotion, not only for the benefit of the actor, but also to perform one's assigned role in a way that secures the validation of relevant audiences. This need not imply a heartless "masking" of the raw anguish of loss to garner social approval, but rather an ability to manage one's level of distress to reestablish a sustainable personal equilibrium as well as to seek a new relational harmony with others and adequate performance of essential life tasks. The delicate interplay of intrapersonal and interpersonal mood management is clearly reflected in studies of grieving families, where bereaved parents, for example, struggle to balance fidelity to their grief with their ongoing efforts to parent their surviving children (Buckle & Fleming, 2010). More generally, contemporary theories such as the Dual Process Model (Stroebe & Schut, 1999) recognize that oscillation between attention to "grief work" and restoration of engagement with the outer world is part and parcel of post-loss adaptation.

Becoming an effective "stage manager" of one's emotions in the wake of loss entails an ability to both *attend* to cresting emotions in order to discover the implicit needs and meanings resident in them (Greenberg, 2010) and to *reduce* the experience and expression of negative emotion to continue to function and promote healing contact with others (Bonanno & Kaltman, 1999). One helpful concept for clinicians partnering with clients in this quest is that of the *window of tolerance* for negative emotion (Ogden, 2010), which posits that effective interventions need to steer between the threshold of insufficient arousal to foster change, and the upper limit of overwhelming arousal that could disable coping and processing, resulting in experiential avoidance. This suggests, for example, that therapists coaching clients to engage in emotional journaling about the loss need to attend to the conditions of safety that would permit the bereaved to draw close to their grief, with a clear time limit or "exit strategy" (e.g., segueing into exercise, visiting with a friend) before doing so. Gradually the goal would be to increase clients' tolerance for "staying with" negative emotion in order to harvest its affirmative lessons, as well as their skills in setting such emotion aside temporarily to make space for other constructive feelings and actions.

A further principle that can guide this work arises from research on *self-distancing*. Self-distancing refers to the capacity to explore one's experience from a less ego-bound vantage point, one that permits one to reconstrue an experience, rather than simply recount it in a ruminative fashion (Kross & Ayduk, 2010). For example, ample evidence demonstrates that when people are asked to write about their feelings concerning a negative experience from a more detached, "big picture" perspective ("Visualize your experience from the viewpoint of a 'fly on the wall,' trying to understand your distant self's feelings...") rather an immersed perspective ("Visualize the experience and your feelings concretely, through your own eyes..."), they are more likely to make meaning of the experience, reduce the intensity of their negative affect, and avoid prolonged rumination. This suggests that therapeutic methods that foster this sort of adaptive self-reflection could play a role in both modulating grief and promoting sense-making about the loss. One narrative technique that is in keeping with this goal is the *loss characterization* (Neimeyer, 2002). This technique encourages the client to write about his or her identity in the wake of the loss, but to do so from a self-distanced standpoint, as seen through the eyes of a compassionate friend, rather than through the eyes of a critic or from an emotionally immersed perspective.

More generally, mindfulness methods that promote meditation on grief-related emotions without attaching to them can serve a similar purpose, widening the window of tolerance for such affect on the part of both clients and therapists, and enhancing their attention to the present moment (Cacciatore & Flint, in press).

Clinician's Toolbox: The Loss Characterization

As a guide to adaptive self-reflection on a loss experience, a client can be asked to write about his or her identity reconstruction in the aftermath of bereavement, perhaps sharing it with a therapist or other members of a bereavement support group for further processing. The instructional set for this open-ended writing invites the writer to consider the self from the standpoint of an imagined friend who adopts a compassionate and knowledgeable stance, rather than to write from a self-critical or emotionally immersed experience about the changes wrought by the bereavement. A typical response consists of about two pages of writing. Simple instructions, printed at the top of a sheet of blank paper, follow.

In the space that follows, please write a character sketch of [client's name], in light of her loss. Write it just as if she were the principal character in a book, movie or play. Write it as it might be written by a friend who knew her very intimately and sympathetically, perhaps better than anyone really could know her. Be sure to write it in the third person. For example, start out by saying, "[Client's name] is...."

Further guidelines for reflecting therapeutically on the resulting narrative are provided by Neimeyer (2002).

Recruiting the Company: Grieving on the Social Stage

Just as a theater company has to "try out" and recruit a cast for each play, many grieving people need to recruit the company who will help them with the "performance" of their grief—even when the expression of their suffering is entirely genuine. And just as in the theater, many grievers will find that not all potential players they audition for a role will pass muster, especially in light of evidence that negative "support" figures who respond critically or intrusively may do more to adversely influence the course of the bereaved person's adaptation than positive support figures may do to reinforce it (Burke, Neimeyer, & McDevitt-Murphy, 2010). Attending to the nuances of the client's social interactions, especially with intimate others, is critical to grief counseling and therapy, as they can either advance or impede the goals addressed in the previous two sections. For example, qualitative research on grieving families documents how spiritual, philosophic, or practical meaning making regarding a death can be either supported or contested by different family members (Nadeau, 1997), and how couples mourning the loss of a child may engage in a delicate dance of distancing to mitigate the potential pain of sharing their grief (Hooghe, Rober, & Neimeyer, in press). Such results suggest the therapeutic value of both *talking* and *not talking* about the loss, with permission for both being negotiated in concert with family members.

One practical tool for therapists who are joining with a client to review how well close relationships can accommodate his or her needs following bereavement is the DLR approach offered by Doka. DLR is a useful mnemonic for considering who in the client's social field is a *Doer* (someone who can be counted on to complete a specific task, like assisting with errands or child care), a *Listener* (friends who are empathic and nonjudgmental in hearing what is in our hearts), or a *Respite figure* (someone who is a good "activity buddy," who might accompany us for shopping, having lunch or seeing a movie) (Doka, 2010). To this basic DLR inventory we might add an N, for *Negative relationship*—the kind of people the bereaved person would do well to avoid or engage in only limited ways. More subtly, of course, therapists can assist clients in considering ways to minimize the burden on a limited number of support figures, and how to "titrate" the sharing of feelings and needs so that a potential supporter is not overwhelmed.

Clinician's Toolbox: Grief on the Social Stage

Ultimately, grieving is something that happens between people as well as within them. As a result, grief therapy often needs to help people reconstruct their social world in the wake of loss, making informed choices about who to turn to for what sort of support, and who to avoid. Drawing on Doka's (2010) DLR approach, and adding a simple elaboration to accommodate the reality of negative social relationships, it is useful to review with clients who in their life fits into the following categories:

Doers (D): people who can be counted on to get things done (e.g., assisting with housework; consulting on a computer program)

Listeners (L): friends who can lend a sympathetic ear, without becoming reactive, prematurely advice-giving, preachy, or critical

Respite (R): support figures with whom to engage in specific activities for the purpose of simple enjoyment (e.g., visiting a gallery; exercising)

Negative figures (N): people who are better off avoided, or if essential to interact with (e.g., a critical parent or relative), to engage in limited interaction.

Thinking about *who* to seek out for *what* is critical in rebuilding the world after loss, as turning to those who are likely to disappoint in a given domain is a recipe for pain, resentment, and self-protective isolation. In addition, bear in mind the need to distribute the client's needs across several figures to avoid burning out any one person. Consider the following suggestions:

- Try to identify six people in each category, and program their numbers into the client's mobile phone
- Schedule at least one D, L & R interaction each week
- Play to the strengths of each person; someone good at home repair might be bad company at the symphony; and enjoyable respite figures might be uncomfortable with strong emotions
- Coach the client to actively reach out to help would-be supporters understand their needs, as others often hold back out of a fear of intruding
- Practice assertive responses to critical or nosy people
- Consider the value of *not talking* at times about the loss in regulating one's own emotions and those of the other

Developing Dialogue: Renewing Bonds

Unless they are a troupe of mimes or acrobats, most theatrical performances rely heavily on dialogue to carry the story, build credible characters, and explore their relationships with one another. Likewise, the development of dialogue with others plays a crucial role in bereavement adaptation—*including dialogue with and about the deceased*. In keeping with a continuing bonds orientation (Klass, Silverman, & Nickman, 1996), the goal of grieving might more appropriately be viewed as reorganizing the attachment bond to the deceased than as relinquishing it. Accordingly, research has linked troubling themes in survivors' ongoing dialogue with the dead with the form of their post-loss adaptation. In one intriguing study, bereaved spouses were invited to have one final imaginary conversation with their partner in an empty chair. These conversations were recorded and the dominant themes of self-blame and other blame were coded for comparison with their current self-reports of different forms of psychological distress (Field, Gal-Oz, & Bonanno, 2003). Significantly, those who engaged in dialogues of self-blame (e.g., criticizing themselves for not having cared for or protected the loved one sufficiently) displayed greater grief in bereavement, whereas those whose dialogues featured more other-blame (e.g., accusing the deceased of not having taken care of himself or behaving recklessly) experienced not greater grief, but instead anxiety and somatic problems, even months later. Grief therapy therefore often works directly on promoting healing dialogues with the dead, both to resolve longstanding difficulties in the relationship (Rubin, Malkinson, & Witztum, 2003) and to recruit the symbolic validation of the deceased for the changing meaning of the client's life (Neimeyer, Burke, Mackay, & Stringer, 2010).

Two techniques that can assist the client with these goals are *imaginal dialogues* and *remembering conversations*. In the first instance, a client can be invited to vividly imagine the presence of the deceased, perhaps with eyes closed, or by symbolically placing the loved one in an empty chair in the therapist's office, and then expressing deeply and honestly their feelings and needs, as the therapist prompts, supports, and shapes the client's disclosure. Optionally (but typically powerfully), the client can then be invited to take the deceased's chair and respond, alternating positions until the dialogue moves toward a (temporary) conclusion (Greenberg, 2010). In the context of bereavement, such imaginal conversations can reaffirm or reconstruct the continuing bond with the deceased, resolve troubling concerns about the death or the relationship, such as survivor guilt, and free the client to pursue personal goals of autonomy, effectiveness and relatedness (Shear, Frank, Houch, & Reynolds, 2005).

> ### *Clinician's Toolbox:* Imaginal Conversations
> Imaginal conversations commonly involve enactment of dialogue with the deceased, with the griever playing both roles. Typically, they:
> - Use empty chair or two-chair work to facilitate shift in perspective, as in emotion-focused therapy, with the therapist choreographing the interaction to amplify intensity of contact.
> - Are spoken in present tense, with the therapist prompting for depth and honesty, while staying on the sidelines of the conversation.
> - Are usually vividly emotional, clarifying, and affirming, placing a premium on the experience, followed by further processing between client and therapist about their observations to consolidate learning.
> - May include variations, such as interviewing the deceased, a needy aspect of the self, etc.

A second technique makes use of *remembering conversations* to invoke and support the continued "membership" of the deceased in the client's social world by inviting a description of the loved one, motivated by the same curiosity and interest we might have about a living participant in the client's life (Hedtke & Winslade, 2004). Commonly, the anguish of the bereaved is compounded by their not having any context in which to talk about the deceased because of their own discomfort in introducing them into conversation, or the discomfort of others with their doing so. This sort of narrative work reverses that dynamic, making generous space for accessing, sharing, and extending the loved one's life story, and helping the client cultivate more such contexts in ongoing life. Such work can be begun in individual or family therapy, or in bereavement support groups that start with an invitation to introduce their loved ones to the other group members, and to deepen this sense of connection across the weeks.

> ### *Clinician's Toolbox:* **Remembering Conversations**
> Remembering conversations encourage continuation of the attachment to the deceased, rather than "letting go." Sample questions for prompting this form of healthy continuing bonds include:
> - What strengths did your loved one have that you would like to keep close to you?
> - What were his moments of greatness in life?
> - What would she say about what she appreciated about you during her illness?
> - What did she see in you that let her know that you would be able to handle this situation?
> - How did he hope you would rise to this challenge?
> - If he wanted you to feel closer to him, what might he suggest that you do?
> - Who can help you keep your loved one's stories alive?

Overcoming Complication: Dealing with Prolonged Grief

A final relevant role for the stage manager is dealing with emergencies and complications that arise in the course of a production—as when an actor becomes unable to perform, conflicts erupt within the company, or technical problems threaten the performance. In life as in art, complications can sidetrack or sideline the performance of grief, in a way that requires similar intervention. Chief among these hazards is the emergence of *complicated grief*, a profound, protracted, and pervasive form of separation distress that can preoccupy mourners and undermine their adaptation (Prigerson et al., 2009; M. K. Shear et al., 2011). In essence, the sundered attachment to the deceased can engender a sense of loss of self and security in the social world. The bereaved person is left feeling radically alone in a world that is bleached of meaning, and compromised in his or her ability to perform essential occupational, family, or social roles. When this pattern persists without alleviation for month after month, and as the months merge into years, medical as well as social risks begin to increase, posing a serious threat to health and even life itself. Recent research even suggests that it can foment a later spiritual struggle or crisis for the bereaved who are religiously inclined, for whom complicated grief predicts subsequent perturbation in their beliefs about God's love or power (Burke, Neimeyer, McDevitt-Murphy, Ippolito, & Roberts, in press).

Fortunately, evidence-based therapies are being developed that address this form of prolonged grief, making use of some of the very interventions described above (narrative techniques, imaginal conversations), in combination with restorative retelling (Rynearson, 2006) or revisiting (Shear et al., 2005) procedures for helping clients review and master the story of the loss in less traumatizing ways. A comparison of demonstrably effective treatments involving complicated grief therapy (Shear et al., 2005), meaning-oriented narrative interventions (Neimeyer & Sands, 2011), and cognitive behavior therapy (Boelen, de Keijser, van den Hout, & van den Bout, 2007) suggests that they share the following features: (1) fostering confrontation with the story of the death in an attempt to master its most painful aspects and integrate its finality into the mourner's internalized models of the deceased, the self, and the world; (2) encouraging engagement with the image, voice, or memory of the deceased to facilitate a sense of ongoing attachment while allowing for the development of other relationships; (3) gradually challenging avoidance coping and building skill in emotion modulation and creative problem solving; and (4) encouraging the bereaved to review and revise life goals and roles in a world without the deceased's physical presence (Shear, Boelen, & Neimeyer, 2011). If incorporated in a technically creative, responsive form of grief therapy, these commonalities can serve as principles to guide clinicians helping clients mired in complicated grief to move forward with their lives.

Conclusion

As grief therapy enters its second century of formal development, evidence is mounting that older models such as those casting mourners as stage followers have lost much of their relevance. In the place of this largely passive depiction, contemporary collaborations between theorists, researchers, and clinicians (Neimeyer et al., 2011) consistently cast grievers as active copers, proactively engaging the twin challenges of loss and restoration, biopsychosocial and relational tracks through bereavement, and the reaffirmation and reconstruction of meaning. Adopting the metaphor of mourners as stage managers, I have tried in this brief chapter to offer an orientation to some of these conceptual and empirical developments, and link them to "news you can use" as a bereavement professional. I hope that your experimentation with some of these ideas and methods will enrich your work as they have enriched mine, and that our ongoing dialogue as a community of practice will continue to prompt us toward greater helpfulness to those we strive to serve.

Robert A. Neimeyer, PhD, *is a professor of psychology, University of Memphis, where he also maintains an active clinical practice. Neimeyer has published 25 books, including* Grief and Bereavement in Contemporary Society: Bridging Research and Practice, *and serves as editor of the journal* Death Studies. *The author of over 350 articles and book chapters and a frequent workshop presenter, he is currently working to advance a more adequate theory of grieving as a meaning-making process. Neimeyer served as president of the Association for Death Education and Counseling and Chair of the International Work Group for Death, Dying, and Bereavement. In recognition of his scholarly contributions, he has been granted the Eminent Faculty Award by the University of Memphis, and made a Fellow of the American Psychological Association.*

REFERENCES

Boelen, P. A., de Keijser, J., van den Hout, M., & van den Bout, J. (2007). Treatment of complicated grief: A comparison between cognitive-behavioral therapy and supportive counseling. *Journal of Clinical and Consulting Psychology, 75,* 277–284.

Bonanno, G. A. (2004). Loss, trauma and human resilience. *American Psychologist, 59,* 20–28.

Bonanno, G. A., & Kaltman, S. (1999). Toward an integrative perspective on bereavement. *Psychological Bulletin, 125,* 760–776.

Bruner, J. (1990). *Acts of meaning.* Cambridge, MA: Harvard University Press.

Buckle, J., & Fleming, S. (2010). *Parenting after the death of a child.* New York: Routledge.

Burke, L. A., & Neimeyer, R. A. (2011). Spirituality and health: Meaning making in bereavement. In M. Cobb, C. Puchalski, & B. Rumbold (Eds.), *The textbook on spirituality in healthcare.* Oxford, UK: Oxford University Press.

Burke, L. A., Neimeyer, R. A., & McDevitt-Murphy, M. E. (2010). African American homicide bereavement: Aspects of social support that predict complicated grief, PTSD and depression. *Omega: Journal of Death and Dying, 61,* 1–24.

Burke, L. A., Neimeyer, R. A., McDevitt-Murphy, M. E., Ippolito, M. R., & Roberts, J. M. (in press). In the wake of homicide: Spiritual crisis and bereavement distress in an African American sample. *International Journal for the Psychology of Religion.*

Cacciatore, J., & Flint, M. (in press). ATTEND: Toward a mindfulness-based bereavement care model. *Death Studies.*

Campbell, J. (1988). *Historical atlas of world mythology.* New York: Harper & Row.

Coleman, R. A., & Neimeyer, R. A. (2010). Measuring meaning: Searching for and making sense of spousal loss in later life. *Death Studies, 34,* 804–834.

Currier, J. M., Holland, J., & Neimeyer, R. A. (2006). Sense making, grief and the experience of violent loss: Toward a mediational model. *Death Studies, 30,* 403–428.

Dennis, M. R. (in press). Popular culture and the paradigm shifts in grief theory and therapy. *Death Studies.*

Doka, K. J. (2010). Grief, illness and loss. In M. Kerman (Ed.), *Clinical pearls of wisdom* (pp. 93–103). New York: Norton.

Doka, K. J. (2002). *Disenfranchised grief* (2nd ed.). Champaign, IL: Research Press.

Downe-Wambolt, B., & Tamlyn, D. (1997). An international survey of death education trends in faculties of nursing and medicine. *Death Studies, 21,* 177–188.

Field, N. P., Gal-Oz, E., & Bonanno, G. A. (2003). Continuing bonds and adjustment at 5 years after the death of a spouse. *Journal of Consulting and Clinical Psychology, 71,* 110–117.

Fireman, G. D., McVay, T. E., & Flanagan, O. J. (Eds.). (2003). *Narrative and consciousness.* New York: Oxford.

Greenberg, L. S. (2010). *Emotion focused psychotherapy.* Washington, DC: American Psychological Association.

Hedtke, L., & Winslade, J. (2004). *Remembering lives.* Amityville, NY: Baywood.

Heilman, S. C. (2002). *When a Jew dies.* Berkeley, CA: University of California Press.

Holland, J., & Neimeyer, R. A. (2010). An examination of stage theory of grief among individuals bereaved by natural and violent causes: A meaning-oriented contribution. *Omega: Journal of Death and Dying, 61,* 105–122.

Holland, J. M., Currier, J. M., Coleman, R. A., & Neimeyer, R. A. (2010). The Integration of Stressful Life Experiences Scale (ISLES): Development and initial validation of a new measure. *International Journal of Stress Management, 17,* 325–352.

Hooghe, A., Rober, P., & Neimeyer, R. A. (in press). The complexity of couple communication in bereavement: An illustrative case study. *Death Studies.*

Jacobs, S. (1993). *Pathologic grief.* Washington, DC: American Psychiatric Press.

Janoff-Bulman, R., & Berger, A. R. (2000). The other side of trauma. In J. H. Harvey & E.D. Miller (Eds.), *Loss and trauma.* Philadelphia, PA: Brunner/Mazel.

Keesee, N. J., Currier, J. M., & Neimeyer, R. A. (2008). Predictors of grief following the death of one's child: The contribution of finding meaning. *Journal of Clinical Psychology, 64,* 1145–1163.

Kelly, G. A. (1955). *The psychology of personal constructs.* New York: Norton.

Klass, D., Silverman, P. R., & Nickman, S. (1996). *Continuing bonds: New understandings of grief.* Washington, DC: Taylor & Francis.

Kross, E., & Ayduk, O. (2010). Making meaning out of negative experiences by self-distancing. *Current Directions in Psychological Science, 20,* 187–191.

Kübler-Ross, E. (1969). *On death and dying.* New York: Macmillan.

Lewis, L., & Hoy, W. (2011). Bereavement rituals and the creation of legacy. In R. A. Neimeyer, D. Harris, H. Winokuer, & G. Thornton (Eds.), *Grief and bereavement in contemporary society: Bridging research and practice* (pp. 315–323). New York: Routledge.

Lichtenthal, W. G., & Cruess, D. G. (2010). Effects of directed written disclosure on grief and distress symptoms among bereaved individuals. *Death Studies, 34,* 475–499.

Lichtenthal, W. G., Currier, J. M., Neimeyer, R. A., & Keesee, N. J. (2010). Sense and significance: A mixed methods examination of meaning-making following the loss of one's child. *Journal of Clinical Psychology, 66,* 791–812.

Maciejewski, P. K., Zhang, B., Block, S. D., & Prigerson, H. G. (2007). An empirical examination of the stage theory of grief. *Journal of the American Medical Association, 297,* 716–723.

Nadeau, J. W. (1997). *Families making sense of death.* Newbury Park, CA: Sage.

Neimeyer, R. A. (2002). *Lessons of loss: A guide to coping.* Memphis, TN: Center for the Study of Loss and Transition.

Neimeyer, R. A. (2004). Fostering posttraumatic growth: A narrative contribution. *Psychological Inquiry, 15,* 53–59.

Neimeyer, R. A. (2006). Widowhood, grief and the quest for meaning: A narrative perspective on resilience. In D. Carr, R. M. Nesse, & C. B. Wortman (Eds.), *Spousal bereavement in late life* (pp. 227–252). New York: Springer.

Neimeyer, R. A. (Ed.). (2001). *Meaning reconstruction and the experience of loss.* Washington, DC: American Psychological Association.

Neimeyer, R. A., Burke, L., Mackay, M., & Stringer, J. (2010). Grief therapy and the reconstruction of meaning: From principles to practice. *Journal of Contemporary Psychotherapy, 40,* 73–84.

Neimeyer, R. A., & Gamino, L. (2006). The experience of grief and bereavement. In C. Bryant (Ed.), *Handbook of death and dying* (pp. 847–854). Thousand Oaks, CA: Sage.

Neimeyer, R. A., Harris, D., Winokuer, H., & Thornton, G. (Eds.). (2011). *Grief and bereavement in contemporary society: Bridging research and practice.* New York: Routledge.

Neimeyer, R. A., & Levitt, H. (2000). What's narrative got to do with it? Construction and coherence in accounts of loss. In J. Harvey (Ed.), *Loss and trauma* (pp. 401–412). Philadelphia, PA: Brunner Routledge.

Neimeyer, R. A., & Sands, D. C. (2011). Meaning reconstruction in bereavement: From principles to practice. In R. A. Neimeyer, H. Winokuer, D. Harris, & G. Thornton (Eds.), *Grief and bereavement in contemporary society: Bridging research and practice.* New York: Routledge.

Neimeyer, R. A., van Dyke, J. G., & Pennebaker, J. W. (2009). Narrative medicine: Writing through bereavement. In H. Chochinov, & W. Breitbart (Eds.), *Handbook of psychiatry in palliative medicine* (pp. 454–469). New York: Oxford.

Ogden, P. (2010). Modulation, mindfulness and movement in the treatment of trauma-related emotion. In M. Kerman (Ed.), *Clinical pearls of wisdom* (pp. 1–13). New York: Norton.

Prigerson, H. G., Horowitz, M. J., Jacobs, S. C., Parkes, C. M., Aslan, M., Goodkin, K., Raphael, B., et al. (2009). Prolonged grief disorder: Psychometric validation of criteria proposed for DSM-V and ICD-11. *PLoS Medicine, 6*(8), 1–12.

Rubin, S. S., Malkinson, R., & Witztum, E. (2003). Trauma and bereavement: Conceptual and clinical issues revolving around relationships. *Death Studies, 27,* 667–690.

Rynearson, E. K. (Ed.). (2006). *Violent death.* New York: Routledge.

Shear, K., Boelen, P., & Neimeyer, R. A. (2011). Treating complicated grief: Converging approaches. In R. A. Neimeyer, D. Harris, H. Winokuer, & G. Thornton (Eds.), *Grief and bereavement in contemporary society: Bridging research and practice* (pp. 139–162). New York: Routledge.

Shear, K., Frank, E., Houch, P. R., & Reynolds, C. F. (2005). Treatment of complicated grief: A randomized controlled trial. *Journal of the American Medical Association, 293,* 2601–2608.

Shear, M. K., Simon, N., Wall, M., Zisook, S., Neimeyer, R. A., Duan, N., Reynolds, C., et al. (2011). Complicated grief and related bereavement issues for DSM-5. *Depression and Anxiety.*

Stroebe, M., & Schut, H. (1999). The Dual Process Model of coping with bereavement: Rationale and description. *Death Studies, 23,* 197–224.

Wagner, B., Knaevelsrud, C., & Maercker, A. (2006). Internet-based cognitive-behavioral therapy for complicated grief: A randomized controlled trial. *Death Studies, 30,* 429–453.

Index

A

Acceptance stage, 4–5, 8, 131

Acute Crisis Phase, 34

Acute Grief Syndrome, 46

Acute Phase, 37–38

Adjustment Disorders, 104–107

Ambiguous loss, v

American Psychiatric Association, xii, 93, 107

Anger stage, 4, 8, 131

Anticipation, 23

Anticipatory grief and mourning
before and after a death, 24–25
emotional reactions, 21–22
forewarning and, 23
guidelines for care providers, 26–27
historical background, 17
life-threatening illness and, 18–21
non-death related losses, 25–26
in relation to anticipated loss, iv, 23–24

APA. *See* American Psychiatric Association

Attachment bonds, 48

Avoidance of distress, 53–54

B

Bargaining stage, 4–5, 8, 131

Beck Depression Inventory, 103

Bereavement. *See also* Grief; Stage Theory
avoidance of distress, 53–54
Bowlby's understanding of, 47–49
challenges to grief work, 51–52
constructivism, 54–55, 130
continuing bonds, 55–56, 103
defined, 94
Dual Process Model, vi–vii, 53
Freud's theory on recovery, 46
Lindemann's transformation of Freud's theory, 46–47
mainstream views on coping, 45–46
post-death, 11
tasks of mourning, 49–50
trajectories of, 52–53
understanding of, 47–49

Bereavement Related Disorder, 93, 95, 105–106

Bereavement resolution, 45

Blame
other-blame, 144
self-blame, 144

Bonanno, George, 52–53, 113–114

Bowlby, John, 47–49

C

Cancer, Psychosocial Stages of, 34

Care providers
anticipatory grief and mourning guidelines, 26–27

CBT. *See* Cognitive Behavior Therapy

CGT. *See* Complicated Grief Treatment

Chronic depression, 115

Chronic Grief, 95, 114–115, 123

Chronic Phase, 34, 37–38

Chronic sorrow, v

Cognitive Behavior Therapy, 103–104, 120

Common grief pattern, 114

Complicated Grief, xii–xiii, 93–107, 146–147

Complicated Grief Disorder, 93, 96

Complicated Grief Treatment, 103

Compulsive blaming, 96

Conflicted Grief, 95

Constructivism, 54–55

Continuing bonds, xi–xii, 49, 55–56, 103

Continuing Bonds: New Understandings of Grief, xi

Coping mechanisms, 7. *See also* Bereavement

Counseling, supportive, 120

Cross-cultural factors. See Cultural practices

Cruse Bereavement Care, 98

Cultural practices
collective grief, 82
expert companionship and, 66–69
mourning, 81–82
patterning of grief, 78–80

Cultural sensitivity, 82–85

D

Death. *See* Dying; Stage Theory
Death competence, 121
Decline and Deterioration, 34
Defense mechanisms, 7
Delayed grief, 115
Denial stage, 4, 8, 131
Depressed-improved pattern, 115
Depression, chronic, 115
Depression stage, 4–5, 8, 131
Despair phase, 49
Diagnostic and Statistical Manual of Mental Disorders, fifth edition, xii, 61, 91, 93–107
Diagnostic and Statistical Manual of Mental Disorders, fourth edition, xii, 104, 107
Disenfranchised grief, iv
Disinhibited Social Engagement Disorder, 107
Disorganization phase, 49
Distress avoidance, 53–54
Diversity. *See* Cultural practices
DLR approach, 142-143
Doers, 142-143
DSM-IV. See Diagnostic and Statistical Manual of Mental Disorders, fourth edition
DSM-5. See Diagnostic and Statistical Manual of Mental Disorders, fifth edition
DSM-IV-TR. See Diagnostic and Statistical Manual of Mental Disorders, fourth edition-text revision
Dual Process Model, vi–vii, 53
Dying. *See also* Stage Theory
   task models, 31–40

E

Ego integrity, 36
EMDR. *See* Eye movement desensitization and reprocessing
Enduring grief trajectory, 52
Ethology, 48
Existential Plight, 34
Expert companionship, 66–69
Eye movement desensitization and reprocessing, 52

F

Finding the Meaning of Grief through the Five Stages of Loss, 11
Forewarning, 23
Freud, S., iii, 43, 45-46, 84

G

Grief. *See also* Bereavement
   active models of, 135–147
   change in understanding of, iii
   collective grief, 82
   complicated grief, xii–xiii, 93–107
   cultural practices patterning of, 78–80
   defined, 94
   expert companionship, 66–69
   managing distress, 139–141
   meaning reconstruction, 136–139
   multifaceted reactions influenced by development, culture, gender and spirituality, vii–viii
   prolonged, 146-147
   recognition of personal pathways, v–vii
   relationship renewal and revision, xi–xii
   renewing bonds, 144-146
   social support, 142-143
   societal rules for, iv
   stages of, 50–51, 132–135
   Task Model of, 35
   transformation and growth possibilities, ix–xi, 61–71
   understanding of loss, iv–v
Grief, anticipatory
   before and after a death, 24–25
   emotional reactions, 21–22
   forewarning and, 23
   guidelines for care providers, 26–27
   historical background, 17
   life-threatening illness and, 18–21
   non-death related losses, 25–26
   in relation to anticipated loss, 23–24
Grief counseling
   case examples, 121–123
   grievers benefiting from, 113–117
   timing for effectiveness, 117–121
Grief Counseling and Grief Therapy: A Handbook for the Mental Health Practitioner, vi, 35
Grief work hypothesis, iii, 43-44, 45, 49-52
Guided mourning, 104

H

Handbook of Bereavement Research: Advances in Theory and Intervention, 118
Harvard Bereavement Study, xi, 95
High Grief grievers, 115–116, 124
High Growth grievers, 115–116

INDEX

Highly stressful events, 61, 64–66

Hope, defined, 36–37

I

ICG. *See* Inventory of Complicated Grief

Imaginal conversations, 144-146

Impact distress, 34

Indicated interventions, 119

Instrumental grievers, viii

Interpersonal Psychotherapy, 103

Intuitive grievers, viii

Inventory of Complicated Grief, 95, 103–104

J

Journaling, 135, 139–141

K

Kessler, David, 11

Konigsberg, Ruth Davis, 113

Kübler-Ross, Elisabeth. *See also* Stage Theory
background, 3–4
On Death and Dying, iii, 1, 3–4, 50, 77

L

Life crisis, 61, 64–66

Life-threatening illnesses
anticipatory grief and mourning, 19–21
Task Models, 36–39

Lindemann, Erich, 17, 46–47

Listeners, 142-143

Living-dying interval, 33–34

Living with a Man Who Is Dying, 5

Loss. *See also* Bereavement; Grief
characterization of, 141–142
understanding of, iv–v

Loss orientation, 53, 102–103

Low Impact grievers, 115–116, 122

M

Major stressors, 61, 64–66

Meaning reconstruction, 136–139

Middle knowledge, 33

Mitigation and Accommodation, 34

Model of Five Stages. *See* Stage Theory

Morbid grief, 95

Mourning
cultural practices, 81–82
defined, 94
guided mourning, 104

Mourning, anticipatory. *See also* Bereavement; Grief
before and after a death, 24–25
emotional reactions, 21–22
forewarning and, 23
guidelines for care providers, 26–27
historical background, 17
life-threatening illness and, 18–21
non-death related losses, 25–26
in relation to anticipated loss, 23–24

Mourning and Melancholia, iii, 43, 85

N

Narrative psychology, 65

Negative emotion, 139–141

Negative relationships, 142-143

Nonfinite loss, v

Numbing phase, 48

O

On Death and Dying, iii, 1, 3–4, 50, 77

Orders of denial, 32

Other-blame, 144

The Other Side of Sadness: What the New Science of Bereavement Tells Us About Life After Loss, 113, 115

P

Pathological grief, 95

PGD. *See* Prolonged Grief Disorder

Physical tasks, 36

Poe, Edgar Allan, 18–19, 22

Positive transformation, 61–71

Post-Traumatic Stress Disorder, 94-95, 106

Posttraumatic growth, x, 44, 61–62

Pre-death grief. *See* Anticipatory grief and mourning

Pre-diagnostic Phase, 37

Preparatory depression, 4

Prigerson, Holly, 93, 95–100

Prolonged Grief Disorder
arguments concerning designation as a mental illness, 93, 95, 97–98

INDEX

categorization of, 106–107
clinical implications, 103–104
criteria for, 98–100
interventions, 146-147
psychopathology, 100–103

Psychological tasks, 36

Psychosocial Stages of Cancer, 34

Psychotherapy, Interpersonal, 103

R

Rando, Therese, iv, 17, 23

Reactive Attachment Disorder, 107

Reactive depression, 4

Reconstruction of meaning, vii–viii

Recovery pattern, 114–115, 123

Recovery Phase, 37–38

Recovery trajectory, 52

Referrals, 120

Remembering conversations, 144-146

Reorganization phase, 49

Resilience, 114, 122, 133

Resiliency trajectory, 52

Respite figures, 142-143

Restoration orientation, 53, 102–104

Ross, Emanuel, 3

Rumination, 53

S

Sanders, Catherine, ix–x

Saunders, Dr. Cicely, 1, 6

Searching phase, 48

Secondary loss, iv

Selective interventions, 119

Self-blame, 144

Self-distancing, 140

Self referral, 120–121, 123

Separation Anxiety Disorder of Childhood, 100

Separation distress, 94, 99

Social constraints, 66

Social support, 142-144

Social tasks, 36

Socio-cultural factors, 66–69. *See also* Cultural practices

Socrates, 12–13

Spiritual tasks, 36–37

St. Christopher's Hospice, 1, 6

Stage Theory. *See also* Dying
criticisms of, vi, 8–11, 32, 50–51
lessons from, 11–14, 77
model of, 1–2, 4–5
popularity of, v, 5–8

Support groups, 54, 120, 121

Supportive counseling, 120

Symptomatology, 100

T

Task models, 31–40

Terminal Phase, 34, 37–39

Terminality and Preterminality, 34

Thanatology, iii, 31

Traumatic grief, 95

Traumatic Stress Reactions, 106

Treatment-induced deterioration, 117

The Treatment of Complicated Mourning, iv

The Truth about Grief: The Myth of its Five Stages and the New Science of Loss, 113

U

Universal interventions, 119

W

Worden, J. William, vi, xi, 35, 49–50

Work and Social Adjustment, 103

Y

Yearning phase, 48